✠ DONNA-MARIE COOPER O'BOYLE ✠

FEEDING YOUR

FAMILY'S SOUL

DINNER TABLE SPIRITUALITY

PARACLETE PRESS

BREWSTER, MASSACHUSETTS

2016 First and Second Printing

Feeding Your Family's Soul: Dinner Table Spirituality

Copyright © 2016 by Donna-Marie Cooper O'Boyle

ISBN 978-1-61261-835-7

Library of Congress Cataloging-in-Publication Data

Names: O'Boyle, Donna-Marie Cooper, author.
Title: Feeding your family's soul : dinner table spirituality / Donna-Marie
  Cooper O'Boyle.
Description: Brewster MA : Paraclete Press Inc., 2016. | Includes
  bibliographical references.
Identifiers: LCCN 2016026457 | ISBN 9781612618357 (trade paper)
Subjects: LCSH: Families—Religious aspects—Catholic Church. | Dinners and
  dining—Religious aspects—Christianity. | Catholic Church—Doctrines.
Classification: LCC BX2351 .O225 2016 | DDC 249—dc23
LC record available at https://lccn.loc.gov/2016026457

10 9 8 7 6 5 4 3 2

Published by Paraclete Press
Brewster, Massachusetts
www.paracletepress.com

Printed in the United States of America

DEDICATION

This book is lovingly dedicated to my children: Justin, Chaldea, Jessica, Joseph, and Mary-Catherine, and my grandson, Shepherd.

This book is also dedicated in loving memory to my mother, Alexandra Mary Uzwiak Cooper, in thanksgiving for the loving importance she placed on regular dinner times and for the countless seeds of faith she planted and nourished in my heart. Additionally, it is dedicated to my spiritual mother and friend Mother Teresa, in gratitude for the lessons of love and guidance she imparted to my heart and soul.

Photo: Donna-Marie (pregnant with Joseph) with
Mother Teresa at the convent in New York.

CONTENTS

FOREWORD

By the labor of your hands you shall eat. You will be happy and prosper; your wife like a fruitful vine in the heart of your house; your children like shoots of the olive around your table.

—Ps. 128:2–3 NAB

The Scriptures say if the Lord does not build the house, in vain do the builders labor (see Ps. 127:1). When building a home, you simply don't purchase a piece of land and begin construction. You have to build a foundation—you have to dig deep into the ground and build a strong support structure upon which that house will stand firm. Family life is no different. Parents and children must build the foundation of their family on the covenant love of Jesus Christ. In 1 John 4, we see this love in action. John tells us, "If we love one another, God abides in us and his love is perfected in us" (1 John 4:12). God is inviting families to participate in a life of mutual self-gift built on the foundation of love, service, and sacrifice. The strength of covenant intimacy sustains and nurtures families throughout their life together. They learn to see each other through God's eyes, and they should never forget that, even in difficult moments, the Lord is the firm and strong foundation upon which their family is built.

Prayer is both the gift of grace and a response to God's invitation to covenant relationship in the family. Prayer allows families to walk humbly before God in the obedience of faith—to listen to the voice of God and allow that voice to change and shape their lives. Prayer draws them deeply into God's heart so that every day they recommit themselves to a personal relationship of love and life with Him. Families desire communion with God, but they are not fully alive until they are *in* God. "God is love, and he who abides in love abides in God, and God abides in him" (1 John 4:16).

With a little effort, parents can create and maintain a prayerful, Christ-centered atmosphere in the home. The domestic church is the ideal setting for starting faith traditions such as reading and discussing the Sunday Gospel, praying as a family before bedtime, or delivering food boxes to the poor during the holidays—all of which flows from a life of prayer.

The nexus between both covenant love and the life of prayer in the family is the Holy Sacrifice of the Mass. "At the Last Supper, on the night he was betrayed, our Savior instituted the Eucharistic sacrifice of his Body and Blood. This he did in order to perpetuate the sacrifice of the cross throughout the ages until he should come again, and so to entrust to his beloved Spouse, the Church, a memorial of his death and resurrection: a sacrament of love, a sign of unity, a bond of charity, a Paschal banquet 'in which Christ is consumed, the mind is filled with grace, and a pledge of future glory is given to us'" (*Catechism of the Catholic Church*, 1323). Each Sunday, the faithful receive our Lord in word and sacrament, and then live out that reality in the family, the church of the home. Just as the parish family gathers around the altar to be nourished by the Lord, the family at home gathers around the dinner table to be nourished physically and spiritually as they journey together toward heaven.

In this magnificent book, Donna-Marie Cooper O'Boyle shows how dinners are one of the ways in which families provide the setting for each member to discover his or her vocation and mission by following God's plan for his or her life. Through family meals, children will see the faith being lived out in the marriage covenant between their mom and dad, and they will begin to fall in love with Jesus.

Feeding Your Family's Soul will help to create a joy-filled family spirituality that flows from the marriage covenant. This book is an absolutely invaluable resource that will help parents avoid the mistake of outsourcing their responsibility for teaching their children the faith. While important, schools and parishes should not take the place of but rather support what parents are teaching their children at home. This book beautifully demonstrates that a parent's greatest hope for their children flows from their greatest gift to them: teaching their kids by personal witness and example what it means to be fully alive in the Catholic faith.

With so many challenges to family life today, *Feeding Your Family's Soul* gets to the heart of what is most important in the life of the family: keeping Christ as the centerpiece as each family member strives to be holy—to be all that God created and calls them to be. Donna-Marie reminds us that the Lord is the fountain from which families will receive the strength, power, and grace that they need to help each other get to heaven.

Deacon Harold Burke-Sivers
International speaker, author, and EWTN series host
Portland, Oregon

PREFACE

Having grown up in a large Catholic family, I have vivid memories of our family dinners, which consisted of a big bunch of sometimes rowdy kids circled around our modest kitchen table. My mother made sure we said our grace before we dove in to our meal. With eight kids, meals were unpretentious with no frills. What stands out in my mind is the regular dinner time, a valuable tradition my mother insisted on for her family. Because she did, we knew there was comfort in a familial routine; we experienced the stability found in coming together around the table to break bread and converse; and we grew as a family.

It has been my deep desire to write this book for families to encourage them to create their own special memories and form a beautiful tradition, not allowing the demands from the culture and relentless schedules to dictate to them what they should be doing instead of having dinner together—all the while enjoying one another's company.

In my own faith journey, I am very blessed to have shared a friendship with Mother Teresa of Calcutta for about ten years. I'll never forget meeting her for the first time. She looked so tiny! Yet I knew that looks could be very deceiving, and that the humble, unassuming woman—though small in stature and even frail looking—was an absolute powerhouse of faith, hope, and love! She was full of blessed wisdom. And I was a very fortunate and happy recipient of it.

Our very first conversation was all about the family. Mother Teresa told me that my children were very fortunate to live in a family. She was accustomed to picking up abandoned children out of dustbins and taking care of them. Mother Teresa had seen all kinds of poverty and dealt with every sort of need. I told her I felt so blessed to have my children.

Throughout our conversations and times together, Mother Teresa impressed upon me the simple yet poignant fact that "love begins at home." It absolutely must. She often spoke about the importance of being present to one's family and of being sure that all of the needs are met there in the heart of the home before going off to serve God someplace else—whether it be on a committee, in a mission, or wherever.

Mother Teresa was convinced of the power of prayer and the need to pray together as a family. She often quoted Fr. Patrick Peyton: "A family that prays together stays together." Mother Teresa said, "More and more people realize that unless we bring back prayer and love into the family we will never have peace."[1]

I can't help but smile when thinking of a story my friend Fr. Peter told me. A group of seminarians were seated at table about to enjoy a meal together when Mother Teresa suddenly entered the room and saw that one of them had very little on his plate. Most likely, the young man was attempting to use good manners; perhaps he was holding back in a form of penance or mortification. Mother Teresa immediately lifted a nearby large serving platter and in a kind of dramatic motion proceeded to slide an extra-large portion of food onto the young man's plate.

She then, with a sparkle in her eye, looked up at him and said, "You won't be able to take care of the needs of those around you if you are worried about your hungry stomach." Surely this message must have resounded with everyone present, not just the seminarian who had suddenly become the unwitting recipient of Mother Teresa's wisdom and love.

In one of her letters to me, Mother Teresa spoke about becoming a "soul of prayer" and how we should work and pray together to strive to make each of our homes into "another Nazareth":

Fidelity to growing into a soul of prayer is the beginning of great holiness. If we remember "what we do to Jesus—that we do to each other," we would be real contemplatives in the heart of the world. Let us learn to pray and work as Jesus did for 30 years in Nazareth. The life and work; the prayer and sacrifice at Nazareth are so much like what our life should be. That peace, joy and unity that joined the Holy Family together in prayer and work is such a wonderful living example to us. They grew in holiness together. Let us learn from Mary to pray and ask Her to pray that your home will be another Nazareth.

I am very thankful to my mother for forming the tradition of family dinner times in our family. I am also very thankful to my "spiritual mother," Mother Teresa, for encouraging and affirming me in my vocation as wife and mother.

It is my prayer that in using this guide to *feeding your family's soul*, you will endeavor to become souls of prayer, as Mother Teresa suggests, as you go deeper into the faith with your family and pray together in your own domestic church.

INTRODUCTION

Parents know without doubt that it is imperative to feed their family—to nourish them so they can grow healthy and strong. It's our job, after all; we don't need a handbook to tell us about our duty to feed our offspring. It's innate. Parents are all too familiar with the adamant cries from their newborns asking as politely as they possibly can to be fed, and with older children who clamor for food or snacks if we are not quick enough with their meals. It's a fact of life—we all need to eat. And when we're too busy to pause to eat, our growling stomachs remind us to feed ourselves.

There's another kind of hunger for food. Our souls yearn for the spiritual food that is necessary for our spiritual survival. Jesus preached, "Do not labor for the food which perishes, but for the food which endures to eternal life" (John 6:27 NAB). Emeritus Pope Benedict XVI stated in *Porta Fidei*: "We must rediscover a taste for feeding ourselves on the word of God, faithfully handed down by the Church, and on the bread of life, offered as sustenance for his disciples."[2]

The Church instructs parents that the teaching and learning of faith should begin right in the heart of the home: "Parents have the mission of teaching their children to pray and to discover their vocation as children of God."[3] We need to feed our children's bodies *and* their souls. "The home is the natural environment for initiating a human being into solidarity and communal responsibilities" (*Catechism of the Catholic Church*, from here on noted as CCC, 2224).

Additionally, we learn from the *Catechism*: "Through the grace of the sacrament of marriage, parents receive the responsibility and privilege of evangelizing their children" (CCC 2225). And, without doubt, the best possible time to do this evangelization, to help combat all of the ungodly things that come at children from the world, is as soon as possible—while they're young. "Parents should initiate their children at an early age into the mysteries of the faith of which they are the 'first heralds' for their children. They should associate them from their tenderest years with the life of the Church" (CCC 2225). A wholesome family life and early teaching in the faith can foster an interior disposition which will "remain a support for" a living faith throughout the child's life (CCC 2225).

As Christians, we understand that God calls us to be shining witnesses of our faith, which will ultimately help others, too. In order to be salt and light to a hungry world—a living sign of the presence of the risen Lord and a credible witness capable of opening hearts and minds—there's no question about it: we must start in our homes. The firm foundation established in a Christian home spills out into the world as the family grows and is involved in community life.

Yet, in the midst of crazy, hectic schedules, all the while feeling bombarded by the messages of the culture, too, sometimes parents can lose lose sight of, or even forget, the need somehow to carve out essential time to teach the faith to their children.

So many parents today feel stretched beyond measure; they have allowed their kids' evening activities to take on a life of their own. Sometimes parents' own schedules are packed too, and many evenings they find themselves running from place to place. Consequently, they grab far too much fast food and miss out on healthy meals and family togetherness in the heart of the home. Family dinners suffer.

It's no secret that we live in a technology-driven age. Everyone wants to be *connected* and see the latest status updates—so much so that, sadly, people often fail to live in the present moments of family life. It's important to be countercultural in making sure everyone comes together regularly as a family to eat dinner.

It might seem daunting to figure out how to reclaim your family dinner times (if they've escaped you). And how can you possibly carve out time to teach the faith to your children? I believe we can nourish our family's bodies *and* souls on a regular basis, even in busy or chaotic households. Christian parents need to roll up their sleeves and really *be* what they are called by God to be: the first and foremost educators of the faith to their children.

Ready to roll up your sleeves?

Feeding Your Family's Soul provides tangible and creative answers to this challenge. This book can become a vital tool for parents, grandparents, and other guardians of elementary-school- to high-school-aged children, helping them to transform dinner into a distinct time to reconnect with the family, pray, converse, break bread, and share and learn our faith.

Each chapter offers a lesson for each week of the year, which can be read at the dinner table on Sunday (or whatever day works best for the family). The chapter opens with a very brief background for you to read to yourself, followed by a succinct lesson to share with the family. You can teach right at the dinner table. In about ten minutes, the family will have been educated in their Catholic faith while gathered together in the heart of the home. Then afterward, everyone can help with dinner cleanup!

Church teaching is offered in a variety of ways throughout the fifty-two lessons: through stories about the saints, excerpts from the *Catechism*, and real-life scenarios that illustrate the teachings. Each chapter has reflection questions you can ask the children. The family can carry the lesson theme throughout the week by using a very simple suggestion called a "theme extension," as well as by praying the suggested prayer together each day whenever it is convenient to do so. You'll find extracurricular activities and recipes, too.

Even amid the household pandemonium, you'll be relieved to have a sensible way to hold your children's attention and use your time together at the dinner table wisely.

I suspect you will thoroughly enjoy your faith discussions centered around the reflection questions at the end of each short lesson. My hope is that the lessons will stir everyone's hearts to desire deeply to know more about their faith. Lessons learned young will be nurtured more and more as the years unfold.

Allow this book to be the rumbly stomach reminding you to feed your children's souls. But, don't forget to have fun with it, too! You don't have to follow it in any sort of order. You can choose whatever theme you'd like for each week.

May this book be a blessed tool to bring your family together at the heart of the home while growing together as a family and growing closer to God!

———— •—• ————

Education in the faith by the parents should begin in the child's earliest years. This already happens when family members help one another to grow in faith by the witness of a Christian life in keeping with the Gospel. Family catechesis precedes, accompanies, and enriches other forms of instruction in the faith. Parents have the mission of teaching their children to pray and to discover their vocation as children of God.

—*Lumen Gentium*[4]

———— •—• ————

PRAYERS

GRACE BEFORE MEALS

Bless us, O Lord, and these Thy gifts, which we are about to receive from Thy bounty, through Christ our Lord. Amen.

GRACE AFTER MEALS

Many people don't pray a prayer after dinner, although it is traditional after eating to thank God and to remember those who have died. Each evening, try to stay at the table together for the couple of extra minutes it takes to pray this prayer together.

We give Thee thanks, Almighty God, for all thy benefits, Who livest and reignest, world without end. Amen.

Vouchsafe, O Lord, to reward with eternal life all those who do us good for Thy name's sake. Amen.

℣. Let us bless the Lord.

℞. Thanks be to God.

May the souls of the faithful departed, through the mercy of God, rest in peace. Amen.

A PRAYER FOR EVERY FAMILY ON EARTH
by St. John Paul II

Lord, from you every family in heaven and on earth takes its name. Father, you are Love and Life.

Through Your Son, Jesus Christ, born of woman, and through the Holy Spirit, the fountain of divine charity, grant that every family on earth may become for each successive generation a true shrine of life and love.

Grant that your grace may guide the thoughts and actions of husbands and wives for the good of their families and of all the families of the world.

Grant that the young may find in the family solid support for their human dignity and for their growth in truth and love.

Grant that love, strengthened by the grace of the sacrament of marriage, may prove mightier than all the weaknesses and trials through which our families sometimes pass.

Through the intercession of the Holy Family of Nazareth, grant that the Church may fruitfully carry out her worldwide mission in the family and through the family.

We ask this of you, who are Life, Truth, and Love with the Son and the Holy Spirit. Amen.

PRAYER FOR OUR FAMILY
by St. Teresa of Calcutta

Heavenly Father, you have given us the model of life in the Holy Family of Nazareth. Help us, O Loving Father, to make our family another Nazareth where love, peace, and joy reign. May it be deeply contemplative, intensely

Eucharistic, revived with joy. Help us to stay together in joy and sorrow in family prayer. Teach us to see Jesus in the members of our families, especially in their distressing disguise. May the Eucharistic heart of Jesus make our hearts humble like His and help us to carry out our family duties in a holy way. May we love one another as God loves each one of us, more and more each day, and forgive each other's faults as you forgive our sins. Help us, O Loving Father, to take whatever you give and give whatever you take with a big smile. Immaculate Heart of Mary, cause of our joy, pray for us. St. Joseph, pray for us. Holy Guardian Angels, be always with us, guide and protect us. Amen.

RECIPES FOR MEALS AND LIFE!

One time I enjoyed a delightful conversation with a man I sat next to on a flight returning from filming some television shows at the EWTN studio in Alabama. You might be wondering what this has to do with recipes. Well, my seatmate, Bill, and I somehow started chatting about families and the faith. He is Baptist and I am Catholic. It turns out we both wholeheartedly believe in the importance of teaching the faith to our families and of being an exemplary model to them.

Bill shared with me about an older woman very dear to him and his wife. In fact, they affectionately call her "Nonna" as if she were their grandmother. Nonna is from Italy and never shares her famous spaghetti sauce recipe— that is, until very recently when she lovingly gave it to them. It was handed down for generations, and now Bill and his wife feel very blessed to have it, too.

Bill and I began discussing the process of making spaghetti sauce. After admitting that many times when I am in a hurry I open a jar for our spaghetti dinners, I shared vivid memories of my mother's homemade sauce simmering in a big pot on our old kitchen stove. I smiled and told Bill that I wouldn't ask him for Nonna's "famous" sauce recipe, since I knew it was confidential and reserved for family members. He smiled and told me that one of the secret ingredients is the fennel seed she adds to the meatballs. He suddenly looked to be deep in thought for a few seconds, and then he said something quite revealing: "The thing is, you need to keep stirring the sauce."

Nonna's sauce recipe requires a lot of stirring after each new addition to the pot.

"That's the problem!" I quipped. Shaking my head back and forth slowly, I added, "We don't have time to stir the sauce anymore."

Families today have become so busy that often they eat fast food rather than take the time to make a good meal. They wrestle with crazy, demanding schedules. I certainly understand that we can't always be "stirring the sauce," but I think it would be nice to bring some of that tradition back to our hearth and home. We can strive to carve out some time to make special meals.

As you go through the weekly dinner table lessons in this book, you will notice that woven throughout are fun and delicious recipes you can make with your family. Most of them have a little story to accompany the recipe. I sincerely hope that you will also feel encouraged to reach out to your relatives and share recipes to keep family traditions going. It is a wonderful way to stay in touch with those relatives, too. I also encourage you to create your own distinct and memorable stories by spending time cooking together in the kitchen. Don't worry about the mess! Messes can be part of the fun and part of the memories!

Children and grandchildren grow up so quickly, and you definitely want to seize the time now to create those delightful memories with them. Do your best to find time—at least occasionally—to "stir the sauce."

In addition, I'd like to suggest that you take out your good china for these Sunday family dinners. It's something my mother taught me when she was sick with cancer. She said we shouldn't wait for a special holiday or occasion to take out the good china. We need to celebrate our family now. Perhaps you can eat in the dining room that evening rather than at the kitchen table. Go ahead and light some candles, too, and enjoy the special experience together. Be sure to invite our Lord and have fun together learning the faith!

ONE

Learning to Love Our Neighbor from St. Teresa of Calcutta

CONTEMPLATE

Because we cannot see Christ we cannot express our love to Him, but our neighbors we can always see, and we can do to them what, if we saw him, we would like to do to Christ.

— St. Teresa of Calcutta,
Something Beautiful for God [5]

PREPARATIONS

Decide if you'll enlist helpers to assist with making the fun recipe and for help with setting the table. If time allows, read the Contemplate passage above and think about it during the day. Also, read the Dinner Table Teaching in advance of your dinner time.

OPENING PRAYER

(to be read out loud by parent or guardian or by all)

Dear Lord, Jesus, please visit our family, blessed with one another and with food to eat. Please bless our bodies and our souls. Please take care of

those who are lacking in food and do not have a family. *Grace Before Meals.*
Hail Mary.

DINNER TABLE TEACHING
Read the Contemplate passage and this Dinner
Table Teaching out loud to the family.

St. Teresa of Calcutta was a religious sister who founded the Missionaries
of Charity order and devoted her life to wholeheartedly caring for the poor.
She lived the Gospel of Matthew (see Matt. 25:31–46). She knew that Jesus's
words, "Truly I tell you, just as you did it to one of the least of these who are
members of my family, you did it to me" (Matt. 25:40 NRSV), should apply
to all of our lives. Jesus taught us very clearly that whatever we do to others,
we do to Him. Further, he taught us that we will be judged at the end of our
lives by how much we have loved and served Jesus in others. Jesus's words
make it very clear to us how we should behave toward others and care for
the people in our lives. Jesus wants us to treat everyone with His love and
tenderness.

REFLECTION QUESTIONS
Ask the children to share their thoughts.

How can we "see" Jesus in our neighbor?

What are some ways we can love Jesus in our family members and all
those we encounter?

Who in particular do you think you should show extra love to? (For
example, someone you know who may be hurting in some way.)

How can you show them love?

CLOSING PRAYER
(to pray together out loud)

Grace After Meals; Dear St. Teresa of Calcutta, pray for us; *Our Father.*

———❖———

Look over the optional activities below and discuss with the family to see if you can carry them out during the upcoming week.

WEEKDAY PRAYER
Each evening of the upcoming week at the dinner
table, pray this simple prayer.

Dear Lord, Jesus, open our hearts to love more. St. Teresa of Calcutta, help us to be attentive to the needs around us, and show us how to love with Jesus's love. Amen.

THEME EXTENSION
This activity is for anyone in the family, or it can be carried out together.

Sometime this week, surprise someone with an unexpected act of kindness. Ponder this in advance if possible. Will it be a homemade greeting card? Will it be doing something to help another?

Read Matthew 25:31–46 and ponder the words and meaning. Then research St. Teresa of Calcutta's life and share something about her with the family at the dinner table during the upcoming week.

• RECIPE •

Irish Soda Bread

Every year when St. Patrick's Day is coming up, I get a hankering to make Irish soda bread. Each time I make it I think (since St. Paddy's Day falls during Lent) that it really tastes too good for a Lenten bread. I use my friend Mary Maguire's old-time recipe and tweak it a bit. I usually double this recipe to make two loaves: one just to make sure it tastes good and one for St. Patrick's Day!

Ingredients
- 3 cups flour (sometimes I use a wholegrain flour for more nutrition)
- 2 tsp. baking powder
- 1 tsp. baking soda
- 1 tsp. salt
- 1 tsp. caraway seeds (optional)
- 1¼ cups buttermilk (I use milk with a couple of tablespoons of apple cider vinegar mixed in to curdle it)
- ¼ cup butter softened (you can substitute with soy margarine)
- ½ cup sugar (sometimes I use honey)
- 1 egg
- 1 cup raisins (I love to use golden raisins or a combination of golden and black)

Directions

Mix flour, baking powder, baking soda, salt, and caraway seeds in a large
bowl. Cut in the butter until crumbly; stir in the raisins and sugar. Add
beaten egg and buttermilk to mixture; stir until dough clings together.

On a lightly floured surface, knead gently and shape into a ball. Grease and
flour cake pan lightly; place dough in pan and pat to fit pan. Brush top
with beaten egg and cut a deep cross in the top of the bread with a sharp
knife. Don't forget the cross! Bake in oven at about 350°F for about an
hour or until a cake pick inserted in the center comes out clean. Place on
a wire rack, and brush the top with butter. Yum!

Note: Sometimes I substitute soy butter for the butter. I sometimes shape
our loaves into rounds and bake them on cookie sheets rather than in
cake pans—both ways work well. Every now and then I don't put an
egg wash on top. Occasionally, I use half whole wheat flour and half
unbleached white flour to make the bread a bit more nutritious. Also,
I'll let you in on a little secret: I don't usually have buttermilk on hand,
so instead I use regular milk with a couple of tablespoons of cider vinegar
mixed in to curdle it. Don't worry, this is safe, and some recipes give this
option.

One thing I can guarantee is that every time I make Irish soda bread, I
ask myself why I only make this bread at St. Patrick's Day. It tastes so
delicious! Enjoy!

TWO
Living the Beatitudes

CONTEMPLATE

When Jesus saw the crowds, he went up the mountain; and after he sat down, his disciples came to him. Then he began to speak, \
and taught them, saying: "Blessed are the poor in spirit, for theirs is the kingdom of heaven."

—Matthew 5:1–3 (NRSV)

PREPARATIONS

Decide if you'll enlist helpers to assist with making the fun recipe and for help with setting the table. If time allows, read the Contemplate passage above and think about it during the day. Also, read the Dinner Table Teaching in advance of your dinner time.

OPENING PRAYER
(to be read out loud by parent or guardian or by all)

Dear Lord, Jesus, please visit our family, blessed with one another and with food to eat. Please take care of those who are lacking in food and do not have a family. *Grace Before Meals. Hail Mary.*

DINNER TABLE TEACHING

Read the Contemplate passage and this Dinner
Table Teaching out loud to the family.

Jesus taught the Beatitudes in the Sermon on the Mount (see Matt. 5:1–10). *Beatitude* means a state of deep joy and happiness. Jesus impressed upon his followers that authentic Christian discipleship is based on the Beatitudes and that they would be happy in this life and the next if they followed them. He also said that the Beatitudes fulfill God's promises to Abraham and his descendants. Faithful followers of Jesus will enjoy meaningful rewards despite the challenges they endure. Jesus further taught His followers that love is at the heart of all Christian commandments.

The Beatitudes are as follows:

Blessed are the poor in spirit: for theirs is the kingdom of heaven.

Blessed are they who mourn: for they shall be comforted.

Blessed are the meek: for they shall possess the land.

Blessed are they that hunger and thirst after justice: for they shall have their fill.

Blessed are the merciful: for they shall obtain mercy.

Blessed are the clean of heart: for they shall see God.

Blessed are the peacemakers: for they shall be called children of God.

Blessed are they that suffer persecution for justice' sake, for theirs is the kingdom of heaven.

(Matt. 5:3–10 Douay-Rheims)

REFLECTION QUESTIONS

Ask the children to share their thoughts.

What does it mean to hunger and thirst for justice? *Parents, help the kids out with this.*

Who are the clean of heart? Are you?

Do you know anyone who has suffered persecution for justice's sake? Do you think some of the saints might have suffered in this way? Is there someone you can think of who might be currently suffering persecution for being a Christian? *Parents can tell the children about Christians who were persecuted and who are being persecuted.*

CLOSING PRAYER

(to pray together out loud)

Grace After Meals. Teach us, Lord, to follow you always, even when it is difficult, even when we are criticized. *Our Father.*

Look over the optional activities below and discuss them with the family to see if you can carry them out during the upcoming week.

WEEKDAY PRAYER

Each evening of the upcoming week at the dinner table,
pray this simple prayer.

Lord, Jesus, I want to follow You. Lead me so that I may lead others to You. Please bless and give strength to the persecuted. Amen.

THEME EXTENSION

This activity is for anyone in the family, or it can be carried out together.

Ponder someone you know who has been mourning. Devise a plan (simple or more involved) that you can carry out to bring them comfort. It can be as simple as an e-mail or a phone call.

EXTRA CREDIT!

This activity is for anyone in the family.

If possible, find some time this week to read over the Beatitudes again and contemplate each one slowly. If you'd like, imagine yourself sitting at Jesus's feet as He is telling you how to live a life of beatitude. After sitting quietly, praying, and meditating on the Beatitudes, choose one or two that especially seem to be speaking to your heart, and ponder ways you can live them more fully and deeply.

THREE
Doing Small Things with Great Love

CONTEMPLATE

You know well enough that our Lord does not look so much at the greatness of our actions, nor even at their difficulty, but at the love with which we do them.

—St. Thérèse of Lisieux

PREPARATIONS

Decide if you'll enlist helpers to assist with making the fun recipe and for help with setting the table. If time allows, read the Contemplate passage above and think about it during the day. Also, read the Dinner Table Teaching in advance of your dinner time.

OPENING PRAYER

(to be read out loud by parent or guardian or by all)

Dear Lord, Jesus, please visit our family, blessed with one another and with food to eat. Please take care of those who are lacking in food and do not have a family. *Grace Before Meals. Hail Mary.*

DINNER TABLE TEACHING

Read the Contemplate passage and this Dinner
Table Teaching out loud to the family.

St. Thérèse of Lisieux was born in Alençon, France, in 1873, the youngest of nine children. Her parents raised her and her siblings in a holy household, emphasizing the sacraments, family prayer, practicing the virtues, and taking care of the poor and sick. Thérèse deeply desired to become a nun and worked tirelessly to be accepted into the convent. As a young teen, she even begged her bishop and the pope to allow her to enter the convent early.

After much effort and perseverance, at fifteen, St. Thérèse was delighted to be accepted into the convent and later professed as a Carmelite nun. During her prayers and meditations, St. Thérèse came to understand that God wants us all to put our hearts fully into our actions. She took comfort in the words of Scripture: "Unless you change and become like little children, you will never enter the kingdom of heaven" (Matt. 18:3 NIV). She later became known as the saint of the "Little Way" because she preached that "Our Lord does not look so much at the greatness of our actions, nor even at their difficulty, but at the love with which we do them."

St. Thérèse wanted everyone to know that God doesn't expect us to do grand things but rather to do small things with great love. St. Thérèse learned from Scripture that all deeds, even the most perfect, have no value unless they have love. She realized that charity is the great way that leads a soul securely to God. She committed to doing everything with great love.

REFLECTION QUESTIONS

Ask the children to share their thoughts.

How can you put your whole heart into your actions? Name two examples of things you can do differently to please God.

How can you imitate St. Thérèse's perseverance in doing holy things? Why do you think God wants you to do everything with great love?

CLOSING PRAYER

(to pray together out loud)

Grace After Meals. St. Thérèse, please pray for us. *Our Father.*

✦

Look over the optional activities below and discuss with the family to see if you can carry them out during the upcoming week.

WEEKDAY PRAYER

Each day of the upcoming week at the dinner table, pray this simple prayer.

Dear Lord, Jesus, open my heart to Your love. St. Thérèse, please teach me your Little Way. Amen.

THEME EXTENSION

This activity is for anyone in the family, or it can be carried out together.

During the upcoming week, any time the kids feel the need to make a decision about how to act or what to do, encourage them to think, "What would St. Thérèse do?"

EXTRA CREDIT!

This activity is for anyone in the family.

Sometime this week, take a few moments to research St. Thérèse. Share the information with the family at the dinner table one evening.

• RECIPE •

Make Your Own Pizza

It's fun to get the family involved with assembling the toppings.

Ingredients

- about 1 lb. fresh pizza dough or ready-made crusts for as many pizzas as will feed your family (there are a variety of healthy pizza crusts available, as well as gluten-free types)
- about ½ cup of your favorite tomato sauce
- about ¾ cup (3 oz.) per pizza of shredded cheddar and mozzarella cheese (or other favorite cheeses)
- assorted toppings (diced red or green peppers, chopped broccoli, browned and fully cooked ground turkey meat, sliced mushrooms, diced onions, pineapple chunks, and whatever else you enjoy)
- ricotta cheese (optional)
- cooking spray

Directions

In advance, purchase pre-made pizza dough or ready-made pizza crust, or make your own pizza dough by following a recipe. Follow the instructions for whichever crust you decide upon.

Preheat the oven to the appropriate temperature following the pizza crust instructions. Take pizza crusts or roll out pizza dough and place them on baking pans. Spoon on tomato sauce. Spread on toppings evenly. This is the fun part! Sprinkle the shredded cheeses liberally over the other toppings and, if you choose to use it, place spoonfuls of ricotta cheese on top. Bake according to pizza crust instructions.

Serve with a green salad or fresh fruit. Enjoy!

FOUR
The Communion of Saints

CONTEMPLATE

We believe in the communion of all the faithful of Christ, those who are pilgrims on earth, the dead who are attaining their purification, and the blessed in heaven, all together forming one Church; and we believe that in this communion the merciful love of God and his saints is ever listening to our prayers.
—Paul VI, *Credo of the People of God*[6]

PREPARATIONS

Decide in advance if you'll enlist helpers to assist with making dinner and for help with setting the table. If time allows, read the Contemplate passage and think about it during the day. Also, read the Dinner Table Teaching in advance of your dinner time.

OPENING PRAYER
(to be read out loud by parent or guardian or by all)

Dear Lord, Jesus, please visit our family, blessed with one another and with food to eat. Please take care of those who are lacking in food and do not have a family. *Grace Before Meals. Hail Mary.*

DINNER TABLE TEACHING

Read the Contemplate passage and this Dinner
Table Teaching out loud to the family.

As members of the Catholic Church, we are part of a family. It can be comforting to know that we are part of a huge, blessed family stretching around the globe. There are three parts to our family. The Church teaches us about them when it says, "When the Lord comes in glory, and all his angels with him, death will be no more and all things will be subject to him. But at the present time some of his disciples are pilgrims on earth. Others have died and are being purified, while still others are in glory, contemplating 'in full light, God himself triune and one, exactly as he is'" (CCC 954).

We know that those "being purified" are in a place called purgatory waiting to get to heaven. They are referred to as the "Church Suffering." Their suffering is in their waiting to see God. In God's mercy, He created a place for this purification. Souls, once in purgatory, can no longer pray for themselves but often pray for us. As well, we can pray for the souls in purgatory so they get to heaven sooner.

The "Communion of Saints" are in heaven and are with God! These souls are referred to as the "Church Triumphant." They are enjoying the beatific vision in heaven, where they will remain forever.

We are the "pilgrims on earth," referred to as the "Church Militant." We busy ourselves at working out our salvation so that we will one day be happy in heaven with God. That is truly the purpose of our lives on earth.

While we are here on earth, we can call upon the saints in heaven to help us. St. Dominic, when he was dying, told his brother Dominicans, "Do not weep, for I shall be more useful to you after my death and I shall help you then more effectively than during my life." He knew the power of saints' intercessions for the "pilgrims on earth." Similarly, St. Thérèse said, "I want to spend my heaven in doing good on earth." She knew that her life would not be over when she died. She would simply be in another state of the Communion of Saints and could pray for the faithful here on earth.

REFLECTION QUESTIONS
Ask the children to share their thoughts.

Name three ways that you can work out your salvation on earth.

How can you ask a saint to help you?

Why do you think that St. Dominic and St. Thérèse of Lisieux were happy about dying and praying for others once they reached heaven?

CLOSING PRAYER
(to pray together out loud)

Grace After Meals. All of the souls in purgatory and saints in heaven, please pray for us. *Our Father.*

———

Look over the optional activities below and discuss with the family to see if you can carry them out during the upcoming week.

WEEKDAY PRAYER
Each day of the upcoming week at the dinner table,
pray this simple prayer.

Dear Lord, Jesus, open my heart to Your love. Help me to be more appreciative of being a family member in the Communion of Saints. Help me to live my life so I can become a saint in heaven one day. Amen.

THEME EXTENSION

This activity is for anyone in the family, or it can be carried out together.

During the upcoming week, choose one or more of the following undertakings:

- Make a point of praying for the souls in purgatory (more than just in the prayer after dinner).
- Ask for the intercession of the saints for a person you know who needs help and prayers.
- Think of a way that you can help inspire someone who might be struggling on his or her journey of faith.

EXTRA CREDIT!

This activity is for anyone in the family.

Take a few moments to research any saint and share the information with your family at the dinner table sometime in the upcoming week.

FIVE
Learning Humility from St. Catherine Labouré

CONTEMPLATE

I knew nothing. I was nothing. For this reason God picked
me out.

—St. Catherine Labouré[7]

PREPARATIONS

*Decide in advance if you'll enlist helpers to assist with making dinner and
for help with setting the table. If time allows, read the Contemplate passage and
think about it during the day. Also, read the Dinner Table Teaching in advance
of your dinner time.*

OPENING PRAYER

(to be read out loud by parent or guardian or by all)

Dear Lord, Jesus, please visit our family, blessed with one another and
with food to eat. Please take care of those who are lacking in food and do
not have a family. *Grace Before Meals. Hail Mary.*

DINNER TABLE TEACHING

Read the Contemplate passage and this Dinner
Table Teaching out loud to the family.

St. Catherine Labouré was born in 1806 in the quaint little village of Fain, in the Burgundy region of France. She grew up in a large family and was affectionately nicknamed Zoe. When she was a child, her mother died, and Zoe asked the Blessed Mother to be a mother to her. She worked hard on her family's farm and grew up to become a nun in the order of the Daughters of Charity.

The Blessed Mother appeared to Sister Catherine in a vision and told her, "The good God wishes to charge you with a mission."[8] The Virgin Mary showed her the model for a medal, asking her to have the medals made. Sister Catherine obeyed the Virgin Mary's request, and eventually the Miraculous Medal was made; they are worn by countless people all over the world.

St. Catherine could have boasted about being with the Virgin Mary. She could have bragged that the Blessed Mother of God entrusted her with carrying out a very important and holy mission. But St. Catherine didn't want to draw attention to herself. She shared her mission only with a couple of spiritual directors, keeping it a secret for almost fifty years.

REFLECTION QUESTIONS

Ask the children to share their thoughts.

Why do you think God entrusts certain saints with particular missions?

When God chooses someone for a mission, is it someone proud or humble?

How can you become humble? How can you remain humble?

Why do you think it is good to be humble?

CLOSING PRAYER

(to pray together out loud)

Grace After Meals. St. Catherine Labouré, please pray for us. *Our Father.*

———

Look over the optional activities below and discuss with the family to see if you can carry them out during the upcoming week.

WEEKDAY PRAYER

Each day of the upcoming week at the dinner table, pray this simple prayer.

Dear Lord, Jesus, open my heart to Your love. St. Catherine Labouré, please teach me to be humble and open to listen to God. Amen.

THEME EXTENSION

This activity is for anyone in the family, or it can be carried out together.

During the upcoming week, try to be more aware of times you boast or feel tempted to boast. Try your best to pause and say a prayer asking God to help you to become more humble. Being humble is not easy, but you can do it with prayer and determination.

EXTRA CREDIT!

This activity is for anyone in the family.

Some time this week, take a few moments to learn more about the Miraculous Medal and share the information with your family.

———

SIX
The Consecrated Life

CONTEMPLATE

To follow and imitate Christ more nearly and to manifest more clearly his self-emptying is to be more deeply present to one's contemporaries, in the heart of Christ. For those who are on this "narrower" path encourage their brethren by their example, and bear striking witness "that the world cannot be transfigured and offered to God without the spirit of the Beatitudes."

—CCC 932

PREPARATIONS

Decide in advance if you'll enlist helpers to assist with making the recipe below and for help with setting the table. If time allows, read the Contemplate passage and think about it during the day. Also, read the Dinner Table Teaching in advance of your dinner time.

OPENING PRAYER

(to be read out loud by parent or guardian or by all)

Dear Lord, Jesus, please visit our family, blessed with one another and with food to eat. Please take care of those who are lacking in food and do not have a family. *Grace Before Meals. Hail Mary.*

DINNER TABLE TEACHING

Read the Contemplate passage and this Dinner
Table Teaching out loud to the family.

There are many forms of consecrated life in the Church. The *Catechism* teaches:

> Already dedicated to him through Baptism, the person who surrenders himself to the God he loves above all else thereby consecrates himself more intimately to God's service and to the good of the Church. By this state of life consecrated to God, the Church manifests Christ and shows us how the Holy Spirit acts so wonderfully in her. And so the first mission of those who profess the evangelical counsels is to live out their consecration. Moreover, "since members of institutes of consecrated life dedicate themselves through their consecration to the service of the Church they are obliged in a special manner to engage in missionary work, in accord with the character of the institute." (CCC 931)

Some forms of consecrated life are for the laity, and some are for sacred ministers. The Lord calls many to become consecrated to Him in a formal way, but He calls everyone to consecrate himself or herself to Him and to serve God and the Church. Everyone should pray and ask for guidance to know God's call.

REFLECTION QUESTIONS

Ask the children to share their thoughts.

Have you seen someone who is consecrated—a priest, a nun, or someone else?

What do you think it takes to become consecrated?

Would you like to become consecrated to the Lord one day?

CLOSING PRAYER

(to pray together out loud)

Grace After Meals. All of the angels and saints, please pray for us. *Our Father.*

Look over the optional activities below and discuss with the family to see if you can carry them out during the upcoming week.

WEEKDAY PRAYER

Each day of the upcoming week at the dinner table, pray this simple prayer.

Dear Lord, Jesus, open my heart to Your love. Show me ways to come closer to You. Amen.

THEME EXTENSION

This activity is for anyone in the family, or it can be carried out together.

During the upcoming week, make a special greeting card and give or send it to someone you know who is consecrated, thanking that person for his or her "yes" to God. Surely this will be a welcome surprise.

EXTRA CREDIT!

This activity is for the entire family.

Sometime this week, take a few moments to get in touch with a relative and arrange for a time in the near future to gather for a meal.

Easy and Healthy Yogurt Dessert Parfait

You can make this super easy dessert, which is not only yummy but also healthy, with the kids for lunch or for dessert after dinner.

Ingredients
- French vanilla or plain yogurt (as much as will feed your family)
- fresh or frozen berries
- 1 to 3 bananas (depending on your family's size)
- your favorite granola (being mindful of nuts and the possible choking hazard with little ones)

Directions

Place a few spoonfuls of yogurt in the bottom of several parfait glasses or bowls (enough for each member of the family).

Wash the berries, if fresh. Slice the bananas and layer them with the berries along with the yogurt.

Top the yogurt and fruit with a natural granola. (My favorite is Bear Naked Fruit and Nutty, or sometimes I make my own.) The younger children might not want granola in their parfait.

Voilà! Within a few minutes' time, you have delicious yet healthy parfaits that will please even the fussiest of eaters!

Enjoy this recipe for your dessert tonight or eat it as a lunch.

SEVEN
Learning Courage from St. Maximilian Kolbe

CONTEMPLATE

Let us remember that love lives through sacrifice and is nourished by giving. . . . Without sacrifice there is no love.

—St. Maximilian Kolbe

PREPARATIONS

Decide in advance if you'll enlist helpers to assist with making the recipe below and for help with setting the table. If time allows, read the Contemplate passage and think about it during the day. Also, read the Dinner Table Teaching in advance of your dinner time.

OPENING PRAYER
(to be read out loud by parent or guardian or by all)

Dear Lord, Jesus, please visit our family, blessed with one another and with food to eat. Please take care of those who are lacking in food and do not have a family. *Grace Before Meals. Hail Mary.*

DINNER TABLE TEACHING
Read the Contemplate passage and this Dinner Table Teaching out loud to the family.

St. Maximilian Kolbe was born in Poland in 1894 and baptized as Raymond. For a time when growing up, he was interested in the military. But eventually he and all of his siblings entered religious life, after which his parents entered, too. Raymond would fight spiritual battles, not military ones, for the rest of his life.

Raymond studied theology and philosophy and was ordained a priest in 1918, taking the name Maximilian. He was very devoted to the Blessed Mother. Along with six other men, Fr. Maximilian founded the Crusade of Mary Immaculate (Militia Immaculatae), with the aim of "bringing all men to love Mary Immaculate."

Fr. Maximilian suffered from poor health and tuberculosis, but his ill health would not slow him down—he continued to teach the faith and fight heresy. And he began to spread Church teaching and inspiration through the printing presses. In 1922 Fr. Maximilian began publishing a magazine called *Knight of the Immaculata* in Kraków, "to illuminate the truth and show the true way to happiness."

When World War II broke out, Fr. Maximilian and the friars organized a shelter for Polish refugees, many of whom were Jews. Eventually, the friars came under suspicion, and in 1941, Fr. Maximilian was arrested and sent to the Pawiak prison in Warsaw. He was transferred to Auschwitz, where he would die a martyr's death at the age of forty-seven by giving up his own life so that a prisoner who had a family could be spared. All the while, in the starvation chamber with nine other prisoners, Fr. Maximilian lovingly ministered to the others, putting his own needs aside.

Scripture tells us, "Greater love than this no man hath, that a man lay down his life for his friends" (John 15:13 Douay-Rheims). With God's grace, this is what Fr. Maximilian Kolbe did. He was later beatified and canonized a saint of the Church.

REFLECTION QUESTIONS
Ask the children to share their thoughts.

Why do you think Fr. Maximilian Kolbe was able to continue in his evangelizing efforts even with ill health?

How do you think Fr. Maximilian was able to offer himself for death in place of another prisoner in the concentration camp?

How can you be more courageous in your own life? Give three examples.

CLOSING PRAYER
(to pray together out loud)

Grace After Meals. St. Maximilian Kolbe, please pray for us. *Our Father.*

———

Look over the optional activities below and discuss with the family to see if you can carry them out during the upcoming week.

WEEKDAY PRAYER
Each day of the upcoming week at the dinner table, pray this simple prayer.

Dear Lord, Jesus, open my heart to Your love. St. Maximilian Kolbe, teach me to be courageous for God. Amen.

THEME EXTENSION
This activity is for anyone in the family.

Find ways to be courageous for God. This could mean moving out of your comfort zone to minister to someone—even just with a kind word.

Sometime this week, take a few moments to learn more about St. Maximilian Kolbe and share what you have learned with the family at the dinner table.

• RECIPE •

Pasta e Fagioli in the Slow Cooker

My friend Barb Scholten shares her recipe for Pasta e Fagioli in the slow cooker. Barb was born in Chicago and has lived in Ohio for some time now. I have been a blessed guest in her home and have enjoyed her warm hospitality.

Barb explains, "I have a passion for recipes, and consider it a hobby to collect really, really good ones! So, this has been fun for me, yet challenging in that I have *so* many recipes that have become family favorites over the years; it was difficult to choose a few to send you for your consideration. I tried to find ones that are particularly good for families to prep together, or for family gatherings."

Ingredients
- 2 lbs. ground beef (or ground turkey)
- 1 onion, chopped
- 3 carrots, chopped
- 4 stalks celery, chopped
- 2 28-oz. cans diced tomatoes, undrained
- 1 16-oz. can red kidney beans, drained
- 1 16-oz. can white kidney beans, drained

- 3 10-oz. cans beef stock (or chicken stock)
- 3 tsp. oregano
- ½ tsp. pepper
- 5 tsp. parsley
- 1 tsp. Tabasco sauce (optional)
- 1 20-oz. jar spaghetti sauce
- 8 oz. pasta (uncooked)

Directions

Brown beef (or turkey) in a skillet. Drain fat from beef, and add beef to slow cooker with everything except the pasta. Cook on low for 7–8 hours or on high 4–5 hours. Add pasta for the last 30 minutes.

Serve with a nice crisp green salad and some garlic bread. Enjoy!

EIGHT
Respect for the Human Person

CONTEMPLATE

Before I formed you in the womb I knew you, and before you
were born I consecrated you.

—Jeremiah 1:5 (NRSV)

PREPARATIONS

*Decide in advance if you'll enlist helpers to assist with making dinner and
for help with setting the table. If time allows, read the Contemplate passage and
think about it during the day. Also, read the Dinner Table Teaching in advance
of your dinner time.*

*The Dinner Table Teaching below contains words about abortion and
euthanasia. If you feel your children are too young to learn about this, simply
adjust the teaching so that it is appropriate.*

OPENING PRAYER
(to be read out loud by parent or guardian or by all)

Dear Lord, Jesus, please visit our family, blessed with one another and
with food to eat. Please take care of those who are lacking in food and do
not have a family. *Grace Before Meals. Hail Mary.*

DINNER TABLE TEACHING
Read the Contemplate passage and this Dinner
Table Teaching out loud to the family.

God created us because He loves us. He gives us the opportunity to work out our salvation throughout our lives so that we can be happy with Him in heaven. Our Church teaches us that "human life must be respected and protected absolutely from the moment of conception. From the first moment of his existence, a human being must be recognized as having the rights of a person—among which is the inviolable right of every innocent being to life" (CCC 2270).

Unfortunately, we live in a world where in many places human life is not treated with dignity and respect. Sadly, some countries allow killing an unborn baby in the act of abortion. In some places, acts of euthanasia are performed to end lives. As Catholics and Christians, we can never tolerate this sin. The fifth commandment forbids it. We believe that people do not have the right to end a life.

REFLECTION QUESTIONS
Ask the children to share their thoughts.

What can you do to show your respect for the sanctity and dignity of human life?

Can you take the time to say extra prayers for babies who are in danger of abortion and for the elderly and sick who are in danger of euthanasia?

List three ways that you can teach others about the sanctity of human life.

CLOSING PRAYER
(to pray together out loud)

Grace After Meals. Mother Mary, please pray for us. *Our Father.*

———

Look over the optional activities below and discuss with the family to see if you can carry them out during the upcoming week.

WEEKDAY PRAYER
Each day of the upcoming week at the dinner table, pray this simple prayer.

Dear Lord, Jesus, open my heart to Your love. Dear Mother Mary, show me ways that I can protect human life. Amen.

THEME EXTENSION
This activity is for anyone in the family, or it can be carried out together.

Write a poem about the sanctity of human life and share it with someone.

EXTRA CREDIT!
This activity is for anyone in the family.

Sometime this week, reach out to an older relative and ask him or her to share a favorite family recipe (most likely, you'll make their day by asking!). Write it down and keep it in a recipe box or recipe notebook to be used sometime soon (maybe even with the help of the family). Be sure to include the relative's name with the recipe. By doing this, you will be keeping family traditions alive while staying in touch with relatives.

———

NINE
Learning Obedience from St. Joseph

CONTEMPLATE

A master of interior life, a worker deeply involved in his job,
God's servant in continual contact with Jesus: that is Joseph. *Ite
ad Ioseph*. With St. Joseph, the Christian learns what it means
to belong to God and fully to assume one's place among men,
sanctifying the world. Get to know Joseph and you will find
Jesus. Talk to Joseph and you will find Mary, who always sheds
peace about her in that attractive workshop in Nazareth.

—St. Josemaría Escrivá[9]

PREPARATIONS

*Decide in advance if you'll enlist helpers to assist with making dinner and
for help with setting the table. If time allows, read the Contemplate passage and
think about it during the day. Also, read the Dinner Table Teaching in advance
of your dinner time.*

OPENING PRAYER

(to be read out loud by parent or guardian or by all)

Dear Lord, Jesus, please visit our family, blessed with one another and with food to eat. Please take care of those who are lacking in food and do not have a family. *Grace Before Meals. Hail Mary.*

DINNER TABLE TEACHING

Read the Contemplate passage and this Dinner
Table Teaching out loud to the family.

St. Joseph did not utter one word recorded in Sacred Scripture, yet as the foster father of Jesus his role in salvation history is extraordinary and inestimable. He was constantly doing the will of God and obeying God's instructions. We can learn so much from him. Many times, St. Joseph acted promptly and obediently to help protect the holy family—his wife, Mary, and his foster son, Jesus.

Many of the saints have spoken of St. Joseph's amazing aid. For instance, St. Teresa of Ávila said, "I never asked him for anything which he did not obtain for me." One time, St. Teresa was stricken with a severe illness that paralyzed her, and she begged and begged dear St. Joseph to help her. She was cured of the paralysis and miraculously was able to walk again.

St. Teresa said, "I wish I could persuade everyone to be devoted to this glorious saint, for I have great experience of the blessings which he can obtain from God. I have never known anyone to be truly devoted to him and render him particular services who did not notably advance in virtue, for he gives very real help to souls who commend themselves to him. For some years now, I think, I have made some request of him every year on his festival and I have always had it granted. If my petition is in any way ill directed, he directs it aright for my greater good."[10]

REFLECTION QUESTIONS

Ask the children to share their thoughts.

List two ways in which you can imitate St. Joseph's virtues.

Why is it virtuous to be obedient?

What can you learn from St. Joseph?

CLOSING PRAYER

(to pray together out loud)

Grace After Meals. St. Joseph, please pray for us. *Our Father.*

———

Look over the optional activities below and discuss with the family to see if you can carry them out during the upcoming week.

WEEKDAY PRAYER

Each day of the upcoming week at the dinner table, pray this simple prayer.

Dear Lord, Jesus, open my heart to Your love. St. Joseph, please teach me to do the will of God with a loving heart. Amen.

PRAYER TO ST. JOSEPH

This prayer was found in the fiftieth year of our Lord and Savior Jesus Christ. In the 1500s, it was sent by the pope to Emperor Charles when he was going into battle. It is said to be a powerful prayer especially when said nine days in a row as a novena.

O St. Joseph, whose protection is so great, so strong, so prompt before the Throne of God, I place in you all my interests and desires. O St. Joseph, do assist me by your powerful intercession and obtain for me from your Divine Son all spiritual blessings, through Jesus Christ, our Lord; so that, having engaged here below your heavenly power, I may offer my thanksgiving and homage to the most loving of Fathers.

O St. Joseph, I never weary contemplating you and Jesus asleep in your arms. I dare not approach while He reposes near your heart. Press Him in my name and kiss His fine head for me, and ask Him to return the kiss when I draw my dying breath. St. Joseph, patron of departing souls, pray for us. Amen.

THEME EXTENSION
This activity is for anyone in the family, or it can be carried out together.

Pray the "Prayer to St. Joseph" above each day.

EXTRA CREDIT!
This activity is for anyone in the family.

Sometime this week, take a few moments to read Scripture passages about the Holy Family and pray and reflect on them.

TEN

The Tradition of Prayer

CONTEMPLATE

It is possible to offer fervent prayer even while walking in public or strolling alone, or seated in your shop . . . while buying or selling . . . or even while cooking.
— St. John Chrysostom (CCC 2743)

PREPARATIONS

Decide in advance if you'll enlist helpers to assist with making the recipe below and for help with setting the table. If time allows, read the Contemplate passage and think about it during the day. Also, read the Dinner Table Teaching in advance of your dinner time.

OPENING PRAYER

(to be read out loud by parent or guardian or by all)

Dear Lord, Jesus, please visit our family, blessed with one another and with food to eat. Please take care of those who are lacking in food and do not have a family. *Grace Before Meals. Hail Mary.*

DINNER TABLE TEACHING

*Read the Contemplate passage and this Dinner
Table Teaching out loud to the family.*

The Church teaches us that "prayer is a vital necessity" (CCC 2744) and that "prayer and the Christian life are inseparable" (2745). Prayer is so important to our lives. After all, it is our conversation with God, our Creator. It should always be sincere, and we should pray as often as we can. We are not simply to go to church, then forget about God and prayer when we are not at church. Would we ignore a friend by not taking time to speak with him or her? When we don't pray, we are ignoring God.

In the Contemplate passage above, St. John Chrysostom tells us that we can pray fervently anytime. He encourages us to think about God and to speak to Him as we go about our day—even when we are very busy. Our busy times might even be when it is most important to remember to converse with Him.

St. John Chrysostom also teaches us, "Nothing is equal to prayer; for what is impossible it makes possible, what is difficult, easy. . . . For it is impossible, utterly impossible, for the man who prays eagerly and invokes God ceaselessly ever to sin" (CCC 2744).

Parents can help instill the habit of prayer in their children by encouraging them to pray and by praying with them. Children who grow up with the tradition of prayer will be happier and will be aided throughout life by its firm foundation in their hearts.

REFLECTION QUESTIONS
Ask the children to share their thoughts.

How does prayer help you? Why should you pray?

Do you think your prayers can help others?

Does your prayer make God happy?

What can you do each day to remember to pray more?

CLOSING PRAYER

(to pray together out loud)

Grace After Meals. St. John Chrysostom, please pray for us. *Our Father.*

───────

Look over the optional activities below and discuss with the family to see if you can carry them out during the upcoming week.

WEEKDAY PRAYER

Each day of the upcoming week at the dinner table, pray this simple prayer.

Dear Lord, Jesus, open my heart to Your love. St. John Chrysostom, teach me to pray more. Amen.

THEME EXTENSION

This activity is for anyone in the family, or it can be carried out together.

Try your best to pray for people whom you think are forgotten and need prayers.

EXTRA CREDIT!

This activity is for the entire family.

Sometime this week, if possible, take a few moments to pray to Jesus in the Blessed Sacrament at church or in an Adoration chapel. If this isn't possible, then find quiet time to be with Jesus in prayer wherever you are, maybe even while cooking, as St. John Chrysostom suggests above!

• R E C I P E •

Simple Healthy Salad

You can make this with the kids to eat for lunch or to enjoy with dinner.

Ingredients
- baby field greens or salad greens that you like (enough for the family)
- a few fresh strawberries (sliced) and blueberries
- cheese of your choice (such as Gorgonzola, feta, or blue cheese crumbles, or chunks of cheddar or Monterey Jack)
- 1 can of mandarin oranges (packed in 100% fruit juice)
- a handful of almonds or walnut pieces (being careful not to serve it to the young ones)
- dried cranberries (optional)
- favorite salad dressing (or recipe below)

Directions

Rinse the salad greens and dry in a salad spinner, or by patting with a paper towel. Drain the mandarin oranges, wash the fruit, and slice the strawberries. Assemble the salad: put the greens in salad bowls or on plates, and then add orange slices, slices of strawberries, and blueberries on top. Sprinkle on the cheese, dried cranberries, and nuts. Drizzle salad dressing over each salad just before serving. Enjoy!

• R E C I P E •

Homemade Salad Dressing

My friend Dorothy Radlicz shares her homemade salad dressing recipe. Dorothy says we shouldn't shy away from making our own dressings, because we will taste such a difference compared to store-bought dressings. "I look at cooking as an expression of my creativity, and the side benefit is delicious, healthy food for the entire family and any additional friends. I prefer to use as many organic ingredients as possible since they should be better for you, but you will find, by and large, they also taste a lot better."

Dorothy lets us in on a little secret: "It's important to remember something simple that my teacher chef at the CIA [Culinary Institute of America] once said, 'Everything is a balance of salt, sweet, and sour.' So, keep that in mind when something you are making doesn't taste quite right. Make an adjustment of one of these, and it will be fine."

On the importance of her family dinners, Dorothy notes: "In our house, for generations, we have always put a great emphasis on good food and cooking and eating great meals together, every day. We made sure we would all always come together to eat all our meals, and as our children got older and schedules changed sometimes that meant only dinner would be together." But, still, that would mean "no eating in front of the TV, but around a table so we could and would converse—always starting with a prayer of gratitude for our food."

Ingredients

- 4 tbsp. extra-virgin olive oil (EVOO)
- 3 tbsp. apple cider vinegar (unfiltered) or balsamic vinegar
- 1.5 tsp. agave or honey
- 1 tsp. salt
- fresh ground pepper

Directions

Put vinegar in a bowl and stir quickly while slowly adding olive oil. Add the remainder of ingredients and pour over mixed green salad. Make larger quantities based on quantity of salad. Enjoy!

ELEVEN
Learning Mercy from St. Faustina Kowalska

CONTEMPLATE

I trust in your unfailing love; my heart rejoices in your salvation.

—Psalm 13:5 (NIV)

PREPARATIONS

Decide in advance if you'll enlist helpers to assist with making dinner and for help with setting the table. If time allows, read the Contemplate passage and think about it during the day. Also, read the Dinner Table Teaching in advance of your dinner time.

OPENING PRAYER
(to be read out loud by parent or guardian or by all)

Dear Lord, Jesus, please visit our family, blessed with one another and with food to eat. Please take care of those who are lacking in food and do not have a family. *Grace Before Meals. Hail Mary.*

DINNER TABLE TEACHING
Read the Contemplate passage and this Dinner Table Teaching out loud to the family.

St. Faustina Kowalska wrote in her diary, "And I understood that the greatest attribute of God is love and mercy. It unites the creature with the Creator. This immense love and abyss of mercy are made known in the Incarnation of the Word and in the Redemption [of humanity], and it is here that I saw this as the greatest of all God's attributes."[11]

St. Faustina came from a poor Polish farm family, received very little education, and became a nun. In the convent, she was entrusted with very simple duties, such as working in the kitchen or the vegetable garden, or answering the door. Yet, to this simple unassuming woman, God had entrusted a huge mission of mercy.

On February 22, 1931, Jesus Christ appeared to Sister Faustina and told her about His great mercy for all mankind. Sister Faustina wrote about it in her diary. She said,

> In the evening, when I was in my cell, I became aware of the Lord Jesus clothed in a white garment. One hand was raised in blessing, the other was touching the garment at the breast. From the opening of the garment at the breast there came forth two large rays, one red and the other pale. In silence I gazed intently at the Lord; my soul was overwhelmed with fear, but also with great joy. After a while Jesus said to me, 'paint an image according to the pattern you see, with the inscription: Jesus, I trust in You.'[12]

Jesus told Sister Faustina that God's mercy is greater than even the worst sinner's greatest sins. He continued to give her instructions about the devotion to the Divine Mercy. Sister Faustina's spiritual director instructed her to write it all down in her diary, which later became the book *Divine Mercy in My Soul*.[13]

REFLECTION QUESTIONS
Ask the children to share their thoughts.

Why should you show mercy to someone even if he or she is a sinner and has hurt you?

Why does God want you to be merciful?

What are some ways that you can show mercy to others?

Can you show mercy in your family? That may seem the hardest to do sometimes, but it is very important.

CLOSING PRAYER
(to pray together out loud)

Grace After Meals. St. Faustina Kowalska, please pray for us. *Our Father.*

Look over the optional activities below and discuss with the family to see if you can carry them out during the upcoming week.

WEEKDAY PRAYER
Each day of the upcoming week at the dinner table, pray this simple prayer.

Dear Lord, Jesus, open my heart to Your love. St. Faustina Kowalska, teach me to be merciful. Amen.

THEME EXTENSION
This activity is for anyone in the family.

As situations arise in the household, be mindful of the need for forgiveness and mercy. Make an extra effort to offer these to others. Ask St. Faustina to help you.

EXTRA CREDIT!

This activity is for anyone in the family.

Read St. Faustina's words about the three ways to perform acts of mercy: "For there are three ways of performing an act of mercy: the merciful word, by forgiving and by comforting; secondly, if you can offer no word, then pray—that too is mercy; and thirdly, deeds of mercy. And when the Last Day comes, we shall be judged from this, and on this basis we shall receive the eternal verdict."[14]

Sometime this week, make a point of showing mercy to someone. Is there someone who might have wronged you in some way? Forgive her. Pray for her. Offer a kind word. You can forgive someone in your own heart even if you are unable to forgive the person directly because of distance or circumstances.

Do you know someone who needs comfort? Comfort him. Bring the practice of love and mercy into your lives every day. Scripture teaches us, "Blessed are the merciful, for they shall obtain mercy" (Matt. 5:7).

TWELVE
About Sin

CONTEMPLATE

Sin is an offense against God. . . . Sin sets itself against God's love
for us and turns our hearts away from it.

—CCC 1850

PREPARATIONS

*Decide in advance if you'll enlist helpers to assist with making dinner and
for help with setting the table. If time allows, read the Contemplate passage and
think about it during the day. Also, read the Dinner Table Teaching in advance
of your dinner time.*

OPENING PRAYER
(to be read out loud by parent or guardian or by all)

Dear Lord, Jesus, please visit our family, blessed with one another and
with food to eat. Please take care of those who are lacking in food and do
not have a family. *Grace Before Meals. Hail Mary.*

DINNER TABLE TEACHING
*Read the Contemplate passage and this Dinner
Table Teaching out loud to the family.*

The *Catechism* teaches us, "The root of all sins lies in man's heart. The kinds of gravity of sins are determined principally by their objects" (CCC 1873). Sin doesn't simply happen. We make a choice to sin. We have the power to resist sin by choosing not to get ensnared in it. Even small sins weaken us and can cause us to form habits of sin. When we fall into the habit of sinning, we can cloud our consciences and impair our judgment about good and evil. If we cooperate with someone else's sin, we are responsible for it, too.

The sure remedy for sin is prayer. If we are prayerful, we can become virtuous and earn graces from God to resist sin. If we sin, we must confess it to God and go to the sacrament of confession to be cleansed of sin. God is merciful. There should never be cause to fear the sacrament of confession, because it imparts great grace and gives us peace of heart, a clean conscience, and strength to resist sin.

REFLECTION QUESTIONS
Ask the children to share their thoughts.

Does sin distance us from God and hurt our souls?

What is an example of a little sin that can eventually turn into a big problem when it becomes a habit?

How can you resist sin? List at least two ways.

CLOSING PRAYER
(to pray together out loud)

Grace After Meals. Blessed Mother, Mary, please pray for us. *Our Father.*

Look over the optional activities below and discuss with the family to see if you can carry them out during the upcoming week.

WEEKDAY PRAYER

Each day of the upcoming week at the dinner table, pray this simple prayer.

Dear Lord, Jesus, open my heart to Your love. Help me to turn away from sin. Amen.

THEME EXTENSION

This activity is for anyone in the family, or it can be carried out together.

Create one or more hopeful greeting cards that can be sent to a homeless shelter or a prison.

EXTRA CREDIT!

This activity is for parents or guardians.

Sometime this week, take a few moments to look at the *Catechism* section on sin (Part 3, Article 8). Parents can read parts of it out loud at the dinner table during the week.

• RECIPE •

Picnic Drumsticks

My friend Barb Scholten shares her recipe for picnic drumsticks. She says: "This family favorite is yummy anytime, but especially for summertime picnics! They are great hot, but really yummy the next day, chilled or at room temp on a picnic." This recipe is a favorite for Barb and her family since they love to go on picnics, "whether it's to a local park, on a day trip somewhere, at the zoo, the beach, or the backyard. Picnic drumsticks are always a hit!"

Ingredients
- 1 stick butter
- ¼ cup Dijon mustard
- 1½ cups bread crumbs (can be from bread, or Panko, or store bought, or a mixture of these)
- ½ cup grated Parmesan cheese
- 2 tbsp. chopped fresh thyme (or 2 tsp. dried)
- 1 tbsp. paprika
- ¾ tsp. salt
- ½ tsp. pepper
- 12 chicken drumsticks

Directions

Preheat oven to 400°F. Line two cookie sheets with foil, and spray lightly with vegetable oil. Melt butter with mustard, and stir till smooth. In a separate shallow dish, combine cheese, bread crumbs, thyme, paprika, salt, and pepper.

Dip the chicken drumsticks into the butter mixture (be sure chicken is patted dry beforehand). Next, dip the drumsticks into the bread crumb mixture, pressing to adhere. Arrange on a cookie sheet. Bake until drumsticks are golden brown, about 45 minutes. Serve hot, or let cool, and then refrigerate and enjoy with a picnic tomorrow.

Note: Right out of the oven, these are crispy; they are equally good the next day or two, but not as crispy. Enjoy!

THIRTEEN
Learning to Love the Blessed Mother from St. John Paul II

CONTEMPLATE

Mary is our Mother: this consoling truth, offered to us ever more clearly and profoundly by the love and faith of the Church, has sustained and sustains the spiritual life of us all, and encourages us, even in suffering, to have faith and hope.

—St. John Paul II[15]

PREPARATIONS

Decide in advance if you'll enlist helpers to assist with making dinner and for help with setting the table. If time allows, read the Contemplate passage and think about it during the day. Also, read the Dinner Table Teaching in advance of your dinner time.

OPENING PRAYER
(to be read out loud by parent or guardian or by all)

Dear Lord, Jesus, please visit our family, blessed with one another and with food to eat. Please take care of those who are lacking in food and do not have a family. *Grace Before Meals. Hail Mary.*

DINNER TABLE TEACHING

Read the Contemplate passage and this
Dinner Table Teaching out loud to the family.

St. John Paul II encourages us concerning the Blessed Mother's role in our lives:

> The entire teaching of salvation history invites us to look to the Virgin. Christian asceticism in every age invites us to think of her as a model of perfect adherence to the Lord's will. The chosen model of holiness, Mary guides the steps of believers on their journey to heaven.
>
> Through her closeness to the events of our daily history, Mary sustains us in trials; she encourages us in difficulty, always pointing out to us the goal of eternal salvation. Thus her role as Mother is seen ever more clearly: Mother of her Son Jesus, tender and vigilant Mother to each one of us, to whom, from the Cross, the Redeemer entrusted her, that we might welcome her as children in faith.[16]

St. John Paul II was known during his papacy for having a deep devotion to the Blessed Mother. His motto and coat of arms were dedicated to the Mother of God. He expressed a question that was answered for him in his earlier life:

> At one point I began to question my devotion to Mary, believing that, if it became too great, it might end up compromising the supremacy of the worship owed to Christ. At that time, I was greatly helped by a book by Saint Louis Marie Grignion de Montfort. . . . There I found the answers to my questions. Yes, Mary does bring us closer to Christ; she does lead us to him, provided that we live her mystery in Christ. . . . The author was an outstanding theologian. His Mariological thought is rooted in the mystery of the Trinity and in the truth of the Incarnation of the Word of God.[17]

Throughout his papacy, St. John Paul II gave countless teachings on the Blessed Virgin Mary and wrote much about her. He encouraged the faithful to pray to Mary and get to know her. He was firmly convinced that the Blessed Mother saved him from being killed by the bullets of his would-be assassin. Mary is our Mother. The Blessed Mother will surely bring us closer to her Son, Jesus.

REFLECTION QUESTIONS
Ask the children to share their thoughts.

Do you pray to the Blessed Mother and ask her to help you?

How can Mary help you?

Name three things that the Blessed Mother did.

Extra credit (since the answer cannot be found in the teaching above): What is the name of the angel who appeared to Mary to tell her she would become the Mother of God?

CLOSING PRAYER
(to pray together out loud)

Grace After Meals. Blessed Mother, Mary, please pray for us. *Our Father.*

Look over the optional activities below and discuss with the family to see if you can carry them out during the upcoming week.

WEEKDAY PRAYER
Each day of the upcoming week at the dinner table, pray this simple prayer.

Dear Lord, Jesus, open my heart to Your love. Blessed Mother, Mary, please help us to help others. Amen.

THEME EXTENSION
This activity is for the entire family.

As a family, strive to pray the Rosary or at least one decade together, and offer it for families all around the world.

EXTRA CREDIT!
This activity is for anyone in the family.

Sometime this week, take a few moments to pray this special Memorare prayer to the Blessed Mother.

Memorare

Remember, O most gracious Virgin Mary, that never was it known that anyone who fled to thy protection, implored thy help, or sought thine intercession was left unaided.

Inspired by this confidence, I fly unto thee, O Virgin of virgins, my mother; to thee do I come, before thee I stand, sinful and sorrowful. O Mother of the Word Incarnate, despise not my petitions, but in thy mercy hear and answer me. Amen.

FOURTEEN
About Moral Conscience

CONTEMPLATE

Deep within his conscience man discovers a law which he has not laid upon himself but which he must obey. Its voice, ever calling him to love and to do what is good and to avoid evil, sounds in his heart at the right moment. . . . For man has in his heart a law inscribed by God. . . . His conscience is man's most secret core and his sanctuary. There he is alone with God whose voice echoes in his depths.

—CCC 1776

PREPARATIONS

Decide in advance if you'll enlist helpers to assist with making dinner and for help with setting the table. If time allows, read the Contemplate passage and think about it during the day. Also, read the Dinner Table Teaching in advance of your dinner time.

OPENING PRAYER
(to be read out loud by parent or guardian or by all)

Dear Lord, Jesus, please visit our family, blessed with one another and with food to eat. Please take care of those who are lacking in food and do not have a family. *Grace Before Meals. Hail Mary.*

DINNER TABLE TEACHING

*Read the Contemplate passage and this Dinner
Table Teaching out loud to the family.*

Every single day we need to make decisions—some are very simple to figure out, but some may be difficult for us. The Church teaches that we need to develop a moral conscience, so that we will do what is good and avoid what is bad. We often hear that we must "obey our conscience." But what does that mean exactly? Can we simply do whatever we want and justify it by saying our conscience told us to do so? No, we may not.

We are each responsible for forming a good conscience based on the teachings of God. Parents are responsible for helping form their children's consciences. "A well-formed conscience is upright and truthful. It formulates its judgments according to reason, in conformity with the true good willed by the wisdom of the Creator. Everyone must avail himself of the means to form his conscience" (CCC 1798).

If we have trouble discerning what we should do at any given time, we can pause, pray, and reflect: "The Word of God is a light for our path. We must assimilate it in faith and prayer and put it into practice. This is how moral conscience is formed" (CCC 1802).

When we make sure the Word of God is a light to our path and we do not follow the folly and evil of the world, we will be forming a good moral conscience and will be able to make the right choices. Praying and learning our faith are the keys to doing so. Taking time to incorporate the teachings from this book can be of help as well.

REFLECTION QUESTIONS
Ask the children to share their thoughts.

What are three ways to form a good moral conscience?

Should you follow the advice of your friends?

Where should you seek advice about making important decisions?

What is an example of an important decision?

CLOSING PRAYER
(to pray together out loud)

Grace After Meals. Blessed Mother, Mary, please pray for us. *Our Father.*

Look over the optional activities below and discuss with the family to see if you can carry them out during the upcoming week.

WEEKDAY PRAYER
Each day of the upcoming week at the dinner table,
pray this simple prayer.

Dear Lord, Jesus, open my heart to Your love. Help me to develop a good and strong moral conscience. Amen.

THEME EXTENSION
This activity is for anyone in the family,
or it can be carried out together.

Carry out a simple work of mercy for a family member, neighbor, or friend.

EXTRA CREDIT!

This activity is for the entire family.

Sometime this week, take a few moments to go as a family to Jesus in the Blessed Sacrament and pray for guidance and for everything you need to form a good moral conscience.

• RECIPE •

Overnight Christmas Blueberry-Pecan French Toast

(to be made on Christmas Eve)

I learned of this French toast recipe in an unusual way, which I'll tell you about in a minute. First I'll mention that I love it because all of the preparation is done ahead of time. Then on Christmas morning (or whenever), you simply pop the pan into the oven about 45 minutes before you'd like to serve it. I like to serve this delicious dish with fresh fruit, which can be washed and prepared on a dish and placed in the refrigerator in advance to save you the trouble on Christmas morning. I sometimes also serve fresh muffins along with it. You may substitute a whole-grain baguette in the recipe for added nutrition. You can even use a gluten-free baguette.

On Christmas morning, after placing this pan into the preheated oven, simply set the timer and then go and open your presents! It's so *easy*. That's the idea—to keep it simple and enjoy your loved ones.

Now here's my fun story. One day while at my local food market I came upon an elderly woman (whose name I later learned was Ellen) who was walking around the produce aisle looking a bit lost. She sounded as if she was talking to herself. Actually, she was, as I found out as I approached her.

I asked if she needed any help. She proceeded to tell me that she had been looking for fresh blueberries for a recipe. Since the fresh blueberries were a bit expensive on that late December day, just two days before Christmas, she decided to opt for frozen berries.

I decided to walk with Ellen to the frozen food department on the other side of the store. Ellen and I chatted along the way, and my new friend told me all about this fabulous recipe that she had seen in a magazine, and about how it is assembled on Christmas Eve to enjoy on Christmas morning. I was sold on the idea instantly and grabbed a bag of frozen blueberries myself for my shopping cart. Ellen and I gathered up the remaining items we both would need for the special dish. Before parting company that afternoon, we exchanged phone numbers with the intention to chat again at some point.

Well, we did talk on the phone after Christmas; we compared notes about our delicious overnight Christmas French toast, and we made a date to get together. That was several years ago. Since then, we've been out for tea several times, watched a Christian movie together at the theatre, and chatted about our faith and our families time and time again. I even brought her a rosary from one of my visits to Rome. Though she is not Catholic, she loved it and began praying the Rosary. We are still friends to this day. And to think that we met in a grocery store! I marvel over God's ways. He arranges beautiful serendipitous encounters that turn into meaningful friendships.

I hope you enjoy this recipe. I can't help thinking of my friend Ellen and Christmas every time I make it.

Ingredients

- nonstick spray
- baguette, cut into 20 one-inch slices (I use 1½ to 2 baguettes)
- 6 to 8 eggs
- 3 cups milk
- 1 cup brown sugar (I use honey instead)
- vanilla extract to taste (1 or 2 tsp.)
- nutmeg to taste (I use cinnamon as well)
- 1 cup pecans, toasted
- 2 cups blueberries, fresh or frozen

Directions

Coat a 9 x 13–inch baking pan with nonstick spray, and arrange baguette slices in a single layer in the dish. I usually cheat and make more than one layer. In a large bowl, whisk together eggs, milk, three-fourths of the brown sugar (or honey), vanilla, and nutmeg. Pour the mixture evenly over the bread.

Cover and chill the mixture overnight. There will appear to be a lot of moisture when the mixture goes into the refrigerator, but most of it will soak into the bread throughout the night.

Just before baking, sprinkle the remaining quarter cup of brown sugar (or honey), the pecans, and the blueberries over the top. Bake in a 350°F oven for about 45–60 minutes or until golden and bubbling. (Check it at 45 minutes and keep an eye on it for the remainder of the time.) It should be a light golden brown on top, and the egg mixture should be completely cooked.

Serve with pure maple syrup. For an added treat, heat the syrup with extra blueberries to make blueberry-flavored syrup. You can serve with fresh fruit on the side and breakfast sausage or bacon, too. Enjoy!

FIFTEEN

Learning Forgiveness from St. Maria Goretti

CONTEMPLATE

He loves, He hopes, He waits. Our Lord prefers to wait Himself
for the sinner for years rather than keep us waiting an instant.

—St. Maria Goretti

PREPARATIONS

*Decide in advance if you'll enlist helpers to assist with making dinner and
for help with setting the table. If time allows, read the Contemplate passage and
think about it during the day. Also, read the Dinner Table Teaching in advance
of your dinner time.*

OPENING PRAYER

(to be read out loud by parent or guardian or by all)

Dear Lord, Jesus, please visit our family, blessed with one another and
with food to eat. Please take care of those who are lacking in food and do
not have a family. *Grace Before Meals. Hail Mary.*

DINNER TABLE TEACHING

*Read the Contemplate passage and this Dinner
Table Teaching out loud to the family.*

St. Maria Goretti was born into a poor farming family in Ancona, Italy, in 1890. She was a virtuous girl. When Maria was eleven, a twenty-year-old boy named Alessandro made impure advances toward her. Maria refused to submit to them and tried very hard to counsel the boy against sinning mortally. Alessandro stabbed her fourteen times, and she died a few days later.

Maria prayed for her murderer while she was dying in the hospital. She forgave him, saying she wanted to be in heaven with him one day. Alessandro was sent to prison for thirty years for his crime. He remained unrepentant until three years into his term when he saw a vision of Maria in a dream. She was carrying beautiful lilies to him. He converted to the faith and changed his ways. Twenty-seven years later when Alessandro was released from prison, he went straight to Maria's mother begging for forgiveness, which she gave to him. After that, he became a lay brother in a Capuchin monastery for the remainder of his life.

REFLECTION QUESTIONS
Ask the children to share their thoughts

How did Maria pray for and forgive someone who was so bad to her?

Why does God want us to forgive even in such intense situations?

Why do you think Alessandro converted and changed his ways?

How can you learn to forgive more readily?

CLOSING PRAYER
(to pray together out loud)

Grace After Meals. St. Maria Goretti, please pray for us. *Our Father.*

Look over the optional activities below and discuss with the family to see if you can carry them out during the upcoming week.

WEEKDAY PRAYER

Each day of the upcoming week at the dinner table, pray this simple prayer.

Dear Lord, Jesus, open my heart to Your love. St. Maria Goretti, teach me to pray for those who have hurt me. Amen.

THEME EXTENSION

This activity is for anyone in the family.

Be mindful of times when you feel hurt by others, and pause to say a prayer for the person.

EXTRA CREDIT!

This activity is for the entire family.

Sometime this week, think about making a family cookbook in which you regularly add new recipes that you try out together, especially recipes from your relatives. Take a few moments to ponder ways the entire family can be involved in this project.

SIXTEEN
Being Virtuous

CONTEMPLATE

A virtue is an habitual and firm disposition to do the good. It allows the person not only to perform good acts, but to give the best of himself. The virtuous person tends toward the good with all his sensory and spiritual powers; he pursues the good and chooses it in concrete actions.

—CCC 1803

PREPARATIONS

Decide in advance if you'll enlist helpers to assist with making dinner and for help with setting the table. If time allows, read the Contemplate passage and think about it during the day. Also, read the Dinner Table Teaching in advance of your dinner time.

OPENING PRAYER

(to be read out loud by parent or guardian or by all)

Dear Lord, Jesus, please visit our family, blessed with one another and with food to eat. Please take care of those who are lacking in food and do not have a family. *Grace Before Meals. Hail Mary.*

DINNER TABLE TEACHING

Read the Contemplate passage and this Dinner
Table Teaching out loud to the family.

The human virtues are rooted in the theological virtues of faith, hope, and love. The *Catechism* tells us, "The human virtues are stable dispositions of the intellect and the will that govern our acts, order our passions, and guide our conduct in accordance with reason and faith. They can be grouped around the four cardinal virtues: prudence, justice, fortitude, and temperance" (CCC 1834).

How does one become a virtuous person who will be pleasing to God? We learn from the *Catechism* excerpt above that a virtue is a firm and habitual disposition to do good. Therefore, we must *will* to be good. We must *decide* to be good. We must try our very best to be good. Becoming virtuous is within our power with the help of God's grace, and daily we can pray for the grace we need. Our steady efforts and prayers will indeed help us in the way of virtue.

St. Gregory of Nyssa said, "The goal of a virtuous life is to become like God."[18] As we go about each day, we should be thinking about making the right choices, doing good, and pleasing God. It's so easy to get sidetracked into some temptation or distraction. After all, the messages in our world today beckon to us to focus on our own needs—to take care of *numero uno*. But our Lord instructs us to venture out of ourselves, perhaps beyond our comfort zones, to be virtuous in giving of our love in service to others.

REFLECTION QUESTIONS

Ask the children to share their thoughts.

How many times a day should you practice the virtues? Is there a limit?

Why does God want you to be a virtuous person?

What can you do to become more virtuous and avoid evil?

Give an example of a situation in which you can choose to perform a good act and give the best of yourself.

CLOSING PRAYER
(to pray together out loud)

Grace After Meals. Blessed Mother, Mary, help me to become virtuous. *Our Father.*

Look over the optional activities below and discuss with the family to see if you can carry them out during the upcoming week.

WEEKDAY PRAYER
Each day of the upcoming week at the
dinner table, pray this simple prayer.

Dear Lord, Jesus, open my heart to Your love. Help me to remember that "The goal of a virtuous life is to become like God." Amen.

THEME EXTENSION
This activity is for anyone in the family.

Think about your goals and your actions. Are you becoming like God as St. Gregory suggested? Think about any changes you can make to become more virtuous.

EXTRA CREDIT!
This activity is for anyone in the family.

Sometime this week, take a few moments to read about the virtues in the *Catechism* (see CCC 1803–1845).

SEVENTEEN
Learning Perseverance from St. Monica

CONTEMPLATE

Nothing is far from God.

—St. Monica

PREPARATIONS

Decide in advance if you'll enlist helpers to assist with making dinner and for help with setting the table. If time allows, read the Contemplate passage and think about it during the day. Also, read the Dinner Table Teaching in advance of your dinner time.

OPENING PRAYER
(to be read out loud by parent or guardian or by all)

Dear Lord, Jesus, please visit our family, blessed with one another and with food to eat. Please take care of those who are lacking in food and do not have a family. *Grace Before Meals. Hail Mary.*

DINNER TABLE TEACHING
Read the Contemplate passage and this Dinner Table Teaching out loud to the family.

St. Monica was born in the year 332 in Thagaste, North Africa. Most of what we know about her we learn from the writings of her son, St. Augustine. When Monica was old enough to marry, her parents arranged a husband for her. But Patricius was a pagan. He had a violent temper and was very critical of Monica's Christianity. Even so, she treated him with much patience amid his outbursts and unreasonableness. After years of her gentleness, Monica's husband finally accepted Christianity just a year before his death.

Of her three children, Monica was most concerned for her wayward son Augustine who, though very bright, was involved in carousing and eventually embraced a popular heresy called Manichaeism. Monica shed many tears praying for her son's soul. She fasted and prayed for him constantly. Monica never lost faith that her son Augustine would eventually turn away from his evil ways and come into the Church. Augustine did turn away from Manichaeism, and not too long after, he left his wayward life and was baptized.

From then on, Augustine lived a celibate life and gave himself over completely to the service of God. His mother, Monica, could not have been happier. Both mother and son have been proclaimed saints, and St. Augustine is also a Doctor of the Church. St. Monica's perseverance in prayer and fasting was not in vain!

REFLECTION QUESTIONS
Ask the children to share their thoughts.

Why was St. Monica persevering in her prayers for her husband and her son?

How do you think she was able to continue with her prayers for her husband and son?

What are some ways that you can pray and fast for an important purpose or person in your life?

CLOSING PRAYER
(to pray together out loud)

Grace After Meals. St. Monica and St. Augustine, please pray for us. *Our Father.*

———

Look over the optional activities below and discuss with the family to see if you can carry them out during the upcoming week.

WEEKDAY PRAYER
Each day of the upcoming week at the dinner table, pray this simple prayer.

Dear Lord, Jesus, open my heart to Your love. St. Monica, teach me to pray more and be persevering. Amen.

THEME EXTENSION
This activity is for anyone in the family.

If you experience a time when you want to give up on something, try to pause and say a prayer to be more persevering. You can say to yourself, "What would St. Monica do?"

EXTRA CREDIT!
This activity is for anyone in the family.

Sometime this week, take a few moments to reach out to someone you know who could use some encouragement.

———

EIGHTEEN
Social Justice

CONTEMPLATE

Catholic social teaching is a central and essential element of our faith. Its roots are in the Hebrew prophets who announced God's special love for the poor and called God's people to a covenant of love and justice. It is a teaching founded on the life and words of Jesus Christ, who came "to bring glad tidings to the poor . . . liberty to captives . . . recovery of sight to the blind" (Lk. 4:18–19), and who identified himself with "the least of these," the hungry and the stranger (cf. Matt. 25:45). Catholic social teaching is built on a commitment to the poor. This commitment arises from our experiences of Christ in the Eucharist.

—U.S. Catholic Bishops[19]

PREPARATIONS

Decide in advance if you'll enlist helpers to assist with making dinner and for help with setting the table. If time allows, read the Contemplate passage and think about it during the day. Also, read the Dinner Table Teaching in advance of your dinner time.

OPENING PRAYER
(to be read out loud by parent or guardian or by all)

Dear Lord, Jesus, please visit our family, blessed with one another and with food to eat. Please take care of those who are lacking in food and do not have a family. *Grace Before Meals. Hail Mary.*

DINNER TABLE TEACHING
*Read the Contemplate passage and this Dinner
Table Teaching out loud to the family.*

Jesus instructed his followers to reach out their hands and hearts to the poor. He did this Himself all throughout His sacred ministry on earth. We can and should learn from Jesus and endeavor to aid the poor whenever we can. Further, we are instructed in the Gospel of Matthew to serve Jesus in one another. The Lord is counting on us to do so:

When the Son of man comes in his glory, and all the angels with him, then he will sit on his glorious throne. Before him will be gathered all the nations, and he will separate them one from another as a shepherd separates the sheep from the goats, and he will place the sheep at his right hand, but the goats at the left. Then the King will say to those at his right hand, "Come, O blessed of my Father, inherit the kingdom prepared for you from the foundation of the world; for I was hungry and you gave me food, I was thirsty and you gave me drink, I was a stranger and you welcomed me, I was naked and you clothed me, I was sick and you visited me, I was in prison and you came to me." Then the righteous will answer him, "Lord, when did we see thee hungry and feed thee, or thirsty and give thee drink? And when did we see thee a stranger and welcome thee, or naked and clothe thee? And when did we see thee sick or in prison and visit thee?" And the King will answer them, "Truly, I say to you, as you did it to one of the least of these my brethren, you did it to me." Then he will say to those at his left hand, "Depart from me, you cursed, into the eternal fire prepared for the devil and his angels; for I was hungry and you gave me no food, I was thirsty and you gave me no drink, I was a stranger and you did not welcome me, naked and you did not clothe me, sick and in prison and you did not visit me." Then they also will answer, "Lord, when did we see thee hungry or thirsty or a stranger or naked or sick or in prison, and did not minister to thee?" Then he will answer them, "Truly, I say to you, as you did it not to one of the least of these, you did it not to me." And they will go away into eternal punishment, but the righteous into eternal life. (Matt. 25:31–46)

REFLECTION QUESTIONS
Ask the children to share their thoughts.

Where are the poor in your midst?

Are the poor only people who are homeless?

List the people that our Lord is asking us to help (remember to start with family members.)

What can you do to help others in need? List three ways.

CLOSING PRAYER
(to pray together out loud)

Grace After Meals. Blessed Mother, Mary, please pray for us. *Our Father.*

Look over the optional activities below and discuss with the family to see if you can carry them out during the upcoming week.

WEEKDAY PRAYER
Each day of the upcoming week at the
dinner table, pray this simple prayer.

Dear Lord, Jesus, open my heart to Your love. Blessed Mother, Mary, pray for me that I will be attentive to those in need. Amen.

THEME EXTENSION
This activity is for the entire family.

Make (or plan to make) a dessert or entrée that you can gift to someone in need. Discuss the details with the family, and all pitch in to make it happen.

EXTRA CREDIT!
This activity is for anyone in the family.

Sometime this week, take a few moments to ponder the Scripture passage above in the Dinner Table Teaching (Matt. 25:31–46). Read it slowly, and think about how much you would want to hear Jesus say to you: "Come, O blessed of my Father, inherit the kingdom prepared for you from the foundation of the world." Ask Jesus for His help, and endeavor to live your life serving others and pleasing God.

• RECIPE •

Chicken Tetrazzini

My friend Debbie Burkhart from Missouri shares this family recipe. She says, "Family dinners growing up in our large Italian family were the most important time of our day and we better not be late! The Sunday meal was the most wonderful of all because we were either at our grandparents' house or our own home entertaining grandparents, aunts, uncles, and cousins who were joining us for family dinner."

Debbie knows the importance of keeping traditions alive: "I've tried to carry on that tradition with my own family and have cooked some of the same recipes as my mom."

Being Italian, Debbie considers Sunday "a day of keeping up with our Italian tradition, which includes a pasta dish, breaded baked chicken, a salad, and garlic bread." Debbie and her family have always enjoyed chicken tetrazzini casserole. "It was rich enough to fill up six children and our parents. I also cooked this for my four children and husband. One casserole was enough for the six of us. Three of my children were growing boys!"

Ingredients
- 1 cooked chicken, meat removed from bones and cut or torn into pieces
- ½ cup milk (can substitute low-fat option)
- ½ cup cream (can substitute low-fat option)
- ½ lb. mushrooms
- salt and pepper to taste
- 10 tbsp. margarine or butter
- ½ lb. angel hair pasta
- ½ cups flour
- ½ cup bread crumbs
- 4 cups chicken broth
- ½ cup grated Parmesan cheese (can substitute low-fat option)
- 1 can chicken broth

Directions
Sauté the mushrooms in 2 tbsp. butter or margarine, and set aside. In a bowl, combine the stock from the cooked chicken with 4 cups of chicken broth or water.

Melt stick of margarine or butter (8 tbsp.) in a saucepan and add flour. Mix until smooth. Add chicken broth mixture and ½ cup of cream. Season to taste.

Cook the pasta and drain.

Butter a 9 x 13–inch casserole; add pasta, then layers of chicken and mushrooms. Pour sauce over this, and sprinkle a mixture of bread crumbs and cheese over top. Bake at 350°F until bubbly throughout, which is about 30 minutes. Enjoy!

NINETEEN
Learning to Trust God from St. Augustine

CONTEMPLATE

Breathe in me, O Holy Spirit, that my thoughts may all be holy.

Act in me, O Holy Spirit, that my work, too, may be holy.

Draw my heart, O Holy Spirit, that I love but what is holy.

Strengthen me, O Holy Spirit, to defend all that is holy.

Guard me, then, O Holy Spirit, that I always may be holy.

—St. Augustine

PREPARATIONS

Decide in advance if you'll enlist helpers to assist with making dinner and for help with setting the table. If time allows, read the Contemplate passage and think about it during the day. Also, read the Dinner Table Teaching in advance of your dinner time.

OPENING PRAYER
(to be read out loud by parent or guardian or by all)

Dear Lord, Jesus, please visit our family, blessed with one another and with food to eat. Please take care of those who are lacking in food and do not have a family. *Grace Before Meals. Hail Mary.*

DINNER TABLE TEACHING

Read the Contemplate passage and this Dinner
Table Teaching out loud to the family.

St. Augustine was born at Thagaste on the northern coast of Africa (now Souk Ahras, Algeria) in 354 to a pasgan father and a Christian mother. He received a Christian education but as a teenager ignored his faith and morals and began a wild life of carousing. He lived in politically, socially, and morally decadent times. Augustine and a close friend became involved in a religious sect called Manichaeism. Augustine threw himself fully into the beliefs, devouring all of the books, and ended up defending all of Manichaeism's opinions. He was enamored with this strange religion for nine years to the dismay of his mother, Monica, who prayed for him continuously that he would renounce the cult. Monica was also very upset that Augustine was living an impure life and had an illegitimate child. She prayed for him to turn his life around. This loving mother in tears beseeched her local bishop to help her with her son's conversion. The bishop reassured her that God would not turn his ear from a mother with those tears.

Eventually, Augustine moved to Rome and then Milan. There in Milan he heard the preaching of Bishop Ambrose, which encouraged him to break away from Manichaeism. He took up reading Scripture and was redirected to God. He converted to Christianity at the age of thirty-three. He was a priest by thirty-six and a bishop at forty-one.

St. Augustine has extensive writings to his credit, but his sentiment, "Our hearts were made for You, O Lord, and they are restless until they rest in you," might sum up his and all of our lives. St. Augustine's zigzagging path, getting lost in illusionary pleasures and searching for truth, offers hope to us all. We can be assured that the faithful prayers of his mother, Monica, helped St. Augustine to head in the right direction and work for the Lord. Both Monica and Augustine have been proclaimed saints and Doctors of the Church.

REFLECTION QUESTIONS

Ask the children to share their thoughts.

Why is it important to keep your eyes lifted to heaven and its rewards?

How is learning the faith (as you are doing now) beneficial to your soul?

How can you resist temptation and getting caught up in false teachings? List three ways.

CLOSING PRAYER

(to pray together out loud)

Grace After Meals. St. Augustine and St. Monica, please pray for us. *Our Father.*

Look over the optional activities below and discuss with the family to see if you can carry them out during the upcoming week.

WEEKDAY PRAYER

Each day of the upcoming week at the dinner table, pray this simple prayer.

Dear Lord, Jesus, open my heart to Your love. Blessed Mother, Mary, keep me on the right path. Amen.

THEME EXTENSION

This activity is for anyone in the family.

If you feel tempted to skip your prayers or good works, ask St. Augustine and St. Monica to help you and to give you courage: "St. Augustine and St. Monica, please pray for me and guide me closer to Jesus."

EXTRA CREDIT!

This activity is for anyone in the family.

Sometime this week, take a few moments to reach out to someone who might be struggling to believe in God or who does not believe. Pray for a way to be a good example to that person, showing the love of Jesus.

TWENTY
Learning Steadfast Faith from St. Teresa of Ávila

CONTEMPLATE

One must not think that a person who is suffering is not praying. He is offering up his sufferings to God, and many a time he is praying much more truly than one who goes away by himself and meditates his head off, and, if he has squeezed out a few tears, thinks that is prayer.

—St. Teresa of Ávila[20]

PREPARATIONS

Decide in advance if you'll enlist helpers to assist with making dinner and for help with setting the table. If time allows, read the Contemplate passage and think about it during the day. Also, read the Dinner Table Teaching in advance of your dinner time.

OPENING PRAYER
(to be read out loud by parent or guardian or by all)

Dear Lord, Jesus, please visit our family, blessed with one another and with food to eat. Please take care of those who are lacking in food and do not have a family. *Grace Before Meals. Hail Mary.*

DINNER TABLE TEACHING
Read the Contemplate passage and this Dinner
Table Teaching out loud to the family.

I love St. Teresa of Ávila's explanation above in the Contemplate passage. She certainly makes an excellent point. St. Teresa knew the value of offering our sufferings to the Lord, and she didn't mince words when describing what some might consider adequate prayer.

St. Teresa of Ávila was born into a large family on March 28, 1515, in Ávila, a city in Old Castile, a region that is now part of Spain. She had a Christian upbringing and grew up to be an imaginative and bright child who, along with one of her brothers, was fascinated by stories about saints and martyrs. In fact, when Teresa was seven years old, she and her brother plotted to run away to Africa, thinking they might achieve martyrdom through being beheaded by infidel Moors. Their plan was cut short when an uncle discovered them in the process of running away. Teresa then decided she would become a hermit.

When Teresa was only fourteen years old, her mother died. This affected Teresa deeply, and she decided to beseech the Blessed Mother. She later wrote, "As soon as I began to understand how great a loss I had sustained by losing her, I was very much afflicted; and so I went before an image of our Blessed Lady and besought her with many tears that she would vouchsafe to be my mother."

Teresa's father placed her in a convent of Augustinian nuns for her education, and her uncle introduced her to the writings of St. Jerome. At twenty, she joined the Carmelite Convent of the Incarnation at Ávila.

Teresa experienced many illnesses, including malaria. One time after a seizure, she was thought to be dead. A grave was dug, but Teresa woke from a coma four days later.

God had work for Teresa to accomplish. The determined Teresa undertook to reform the Carmelite order, to restore it to its earlier level of devoutness. Many opposed this, but Teresa felt strongly that God wanted her to do it. Even with ill health, Teresa took strenuous journeys on mules and in oxcarts; she established seventeen new convents for women and fifteen new monasteries for men. Teresa wrote several books on prayer and about her life, which are read by countless people today.

On September 27, 1970, Pope Paul VI proclaimed Teresa a saint and a Doctor of the Church.

REFLECTION QUESTIONS
Ask the children to share their thoughts.

What was special about St. Teresa of Ávila?

How was she able to persevere even when in ill health?

What can we learn about prayer from St. Teresa based on what she said in the Contemplate passage?

What is one virtue that Teresa exhibited that you can try to put into practice in your own life?

CLOSING PRAYER
(to pray together out loud)

Grace After Meals;. St. Teresa of Ávila, please pray for us and help us to be steadfast in prayer. *Our Father.*

———

Look over the optional activities below and discuss with the family to see if you can carry them out during the upcoming week.

WEEKDAY PRAYER

Each day of the upcoming week at the dinner
table, pray this simple prayer.

Dear Lord, Jesus, open my heart to Your love. St. Teresa of Ávila, pray for me. Amen.

Consider praying this prayer of St. Teresa as well:

Let nothing disturb thee;

Let nothing dismay thee:

All thing pass;

God never changes.

Patience attains

All that it strives for.

He who has God

Finds he lacks nothing:

God alone suffices.[21]

THEME EXTENSION

This activity is for anyone in the family.

When you might feel discouraged or perhaps too tired to do God's will, pray to St. Teresa and ask her to pray for you. You can simply pray, "Dear St. Teresa of Ávila, please help me to be filled with a holy determination like you possessed. Please pray to Jesus for me. Amen."

EXTRA CREDIT!

This activity is for the entire family.

Sometime this week, take a few moments as a family to write an encouraging, uplifting poem or note to someone you know who is in the midst of some kind of work for the Church or ministry. Send it to him or her through the mail or by e-mail.

• RECIPE •

Chocolate Sheet Cake

Here is one of my sister Barbara's favorite recipes. She often made this chocolate cake for her children's birthdays when they were growing up. Many times she would decorate the top of the cake with M&M's. This requires a bit more time and effort than simply using a mix, but you will see that it is worth it. Everyone loves this cake!

Ingredients
- 2 cups all-purpose flour
- 2 cups sugar
- 2 eggs, beaten
- ¾ cup sour cream
- 1 tsp. baking soda
- 1 cup butter
- 1 cup water
- 4 heaping tbsp. cocoa powder
- 1 tsp. of salt

Directions
In a bowl, mix together flour, sugar, eggs, sour cream, salt, and baking soda. Set aside. In saucepan, bring butter, water, and cocoa to a boil. Remove from heat. Cool. Stir cocoa mixture into flour mixture and beat with an electric mixer at medium speed until smooth. Pour into a greased 15 x 10 x 1–inch cake pan. Bake at 350°F for 20–22 minutes or until done. Remove from oven and cool for 20 minutes or more before frosting.

Frosting

Ingredients

- 4½ cups confectioner's sugar
- 1 tsp. vanilla
- ½ cup butter
- ¼ cup milk
- 4 tbsp. of cocoa
- 1 cup chopped walnuts

Directions

Mix together confectioner's sugar and vanilla. Set aside. Combine butter, milk, and cocoa in saucepan and bring to a boil. Remove from heat and add to sugar and vanilla. Mix well with electric mixer on medium speed. Stir in walnuts, and then spread frosting over thoroughly cooled cake. Enjoy!

TWENTY-ONE
The Sacrament of Baptism

CONTEMPLATE

Holy Baptism is the basis of the whole Christian life, the gateway to life in the Spirit (*vitae spiritualis ianua*), and the door which gives access to the other sacraments. Through Baptism we are freed from sin and reborn as sons of God; we become members of Christ, are incorporated into the Church and made sharers in her mission: "Baptism is the sacrament of regeneration through water in the word."

—CCC 1213

PREPARATIONS

Decide in advance if you'll enlist helpers to assist with making dinner and for help with setting the table. If time allows, read the Contemplate passage and think about it during the day. Also, read the Dinner Table Teaching in advance of your dinner time.

OPENING PRAYER
(to be read out loud by parent or guardian or by all)

Dear Lord, Jesus, please visit our family, blessed with one another and with food to eat. Please take care of those who are lacking in food and do not have a family. *Grace Before Meals. Hail Mary.*

DINNER TABLE TEACHING

Read the Contemplate passage and this Dinner
Table Teaching out loud to the family.

Jesus told His apostles: "Go therefore and make disciples of all nations, baptizing them in the name of the Father and of the Son and of the Holy Spirit, teaching them to observe all that I have commanded you" (Matt. 28:19–20a).

Baptism is a huge part of our identity as Catholics, and it is one of the three sacraments of initiation in the Church. (The other two are Confirmation and the Eucharist.) The Church teaches us, "Baptism imprints on the soul an indelible spiritual sign, the character, which consecrates the baptized person for Christian worship" (CCC 1280).

When you are baptized, as a baby or as an adult, you receive a truly life-transforming sacrament. Water is poured over your head, and the Holy Trinity is invoked: "I baptize you in the name of the Father, and of the Son, and of the Holy Spirit." Through the water and words, you are initiated into the Church, become a member of the Body of Christ, and receive much grace.

The *Catechism* states: "The fruit of Baptism, or baptismal grace, is a rich reality that includes forgiveness of original sin and all personal sins, birth into the new life by which man becomes an adoptive son of the Father, a member of Christ and a temple of the Holy Spirit. By this very fact the person baptized is incorporated into the Church, the Body of Christ, and made a sharer in the priesthood of Christ" (1279).

REFLECTION QUESTIONS

Ask the children to share their thoughts.

What does it mean to you to be a baptized Catholic?

Why is this sacrament important? List three reasons.

What are some of the things we receive in Baptism?

CLOSING PRAYER
(to pray together out loud)

Grace After Meals. Blessed Mother, Mary, please pray for us. *Our Father.*

Look over the optional activities below and discuss with the family to see if you can carry them out during the upcoming week.

WEEKDAY PRAYER
Each day of the upcoming week at the dinner table, pray this simple prayer.

Dear Lord, Jesus, open my heart to Your love. Please strengthen me in the virtues of faith, hope, and love. Amen.

THEME EXTENSION
This activity is for anyone in the family, or it can be carried out together.

Pray each day for unborn babies.

EXTRA CREDIT!
This activity is for anyone in the family.

Sometime this week, take a few moments to reflect upon your life as a Catholic. Pray for an opportunity to share your faith with someone this week.

TWENTY-TWO
The Sacrament of Confirmation

CONTEMPLATE

Like Baptism which it completes, Confirmation is given only
once, for it too imprints on the soul an indelible spiritual mark,
the "character," which is the sign that Jesus Christ has marked a
Christian with the seal of his Spirit by clothing him with power
from on high so that he may be his witness.

—CCC 1304

PREPARATIONS

*Decide in advance if you'll enlist helpers to assist with making dinner and
for help with setting the table. If time allows, read the Contemplate passage and
think about it during the day. Also, read the Dinner Table Teaching in advance
of your dinner time.*

OPENING PRAYER
(to be read out loud by parent or guardian or by all)

Dear Lord, Jesus, please visit our family, blessed with one another and
with food to eat. Please take care of those who are lacking in food and do
not have a family. *Grace Before Meals. Hail Mary.*

DINNER TABLE TEACHING

*Read the Contemplate passage and this Dinner
Table Teaching out loud to the family.*

Jesus, who was conceived of the Holy Spirit, received the Holy Spirit descending upon him at His baptism by St. John the Baptist. The whole life and mission of Jesus was in communion with the Holy Spirit. Jesus promised to pour down the Holy Spirit upon His Church. He did this first at Easter and then more powerfully on Pentecost.

The sacrament of Confirmation is one of the three sacraments of Christian initiation. (The other two are Baptism and the Eucharist.) The Church teaches that "the reception of the sacrament of Confirmation is necessary for the completion of baptismal grace" (CCC 1285).

Like Baptism, Confirmation "imprints a spiritual mark or indelible character on the Christian's soul; for this reason one can receive this sacrament only once in one's life" (CCC 1317). The sacrament of Confirmation imparts the Holy Spirit and increases the gifts of the Holy Spirit in us. This powerful sacrament unites us more fully to Jesus and "gives us a special strength of the Holy Spirit to spread and defend the faith by word and action as true witnesses of Christ, to confess the name of Christ boldly, and never to be ashamed of the Cross" (CCC 1303).

During the Confirmation ceremony, the bishop extends his hands over those receiving the sacrament and prays:

All-powerful God, Father of our Lord Jesus Christ, by water and the Holy Spirit you freed your sons and daughters from sin and gave them new life. Send your Holy Spirit upon them to be their helper and guide. Give them the spirit of wisdom and understanding, the spirit of right judgment and courage, the spirit of knowledge and reverence. Fill them with the spirit of wonder and awe in your presence. We ask this through Christ our Lord.

—*Roman Ritual,* Rite of Confirmation [25]

Ask the children to share their thoughts.

Why is the sacrament of Confirmation so important?

List three key facts about the sacrament of Confirmation.

How does Confirmation help you to defend your faith?

CLOSING PRAYER
(to pray together out loud)

Grace After Meals. Holy Spirit, please help us. *Our Father.*

Look over the optional activities below and discuss with the family to see if you can carry them out during the upcoming week.

WEEKDAY PRAYER
Each day of the upcoming week at the dinner table, pray this simple prayer.

Dear Lord, Jesus, open my heart to Your love. Holy Spirit, please stir Your gifts in our hearts. Amen.

Also, pray this prayer to the Holy Spirit:

Come, Holy Spirit

Come, Holy Spirit, fill the hearts of your faithful and kindle in them the fire of your love. Send forth your Spirit and they shall be created. And You shall renew the face of the earth.

O God, who by the light of the Holy Spirit did instruct the hearts of the faithful, grant that by the same Holy Spirit we may be truly wise and ever enjoy His consolations, through Christ our Lord. Amen.

THEME EXTENSION
This activity is for anyone in the family,
or it can be carried out together.

Reflect upon the seven gifts of the Holy Spirit: wisdom, understanding, knowledge, counsel, fortitude, piety, and fear of the Lord.

EXTRA CREDIT!
This activity is for the entire family.

Sometime this week, take a few moments to reach out to a neighbor or friend who might be lonely and could use some cheering up. If possible, make an extra portion of your dinner or dessert (with an extra dollop of love thrown in!), and deliver it as a surprise to this person. Have the kids make a sweet handmade greeting card to go along with the gift. If you aren't able to do this during the upcoming week, try to do it soon.

• RECIPE •

Chicken in Tomato Sauce

My friend Rosie Cruz shares one of her favorite recipes. Rosie lives in Texas and was born in Tampico, Mexico, near the beach. I have had the pleasure and blessing of eating at Rosie's dinner table when visiting to speak at her parish. One time Rosie cooked cactus for me! It was my first time eating it.

She says: "My mother always prepared food with the native and seasonal ingredients. I liked all her dishes but especially this one. I learned it because it is delicious, nutritious, and easy for me to prepare."

Rosie's mother worked as a chef in a Catholic school and a hospital, and prepared the food for couples' retreats in their area, sometimes for over a thousand people at a time. Rosie recalls fondly, "Whenever she comes to visit I always ask for my favorite food, and now my children enjoy it too when she cooks for the entire family."

Rosie recommends preparing this dish with natural ingredients "to keep the original flavor."

Ingredients

- 6 chicken thighs without skin
- 2 carrots, peeled and chopped in big pieces
- 2 potatoes, peeled and chopped in 4 pieces
- 1 sweet potato, washed and chopped in 4 pieces with skin left on
- 1 apple, cut into thick slices
- 1 bay leaf
- ½ tsp. thyme
- ½ tsp. marjoram
- 2 garlic cloves, chopped
- ¼ small onion, chopped
- 5 Roma tomatoes, cut up fresh if possible; otherwise canned will work
- 4 tbsp. olive oil
- 1 celery stalk, cut in pieces
- 1¼ cup of water
- black pepper and salt to taste

Directions

Sprinkle the chicken with salt and black pepper on both sides. Heat olive oil in large skillet. Add the chicken, and cook for 5 minutes or until it turns light brown. Turn the pieces over and let them cook for another 5 minutes. Then add ¼ cup of water and cover to cook for about 10 minutes.

Add the sweet potato, carrots, potatoes, bay leaf, and celery stalk.

Blend tomatoes, garlic, onion, thyme, marjoram, and 1 cup of water. Add tomato sauce mixture and apples to the chicken.

Add salt to taste, cover, and let it cook for about 25 minutes more or until the chicken is well cooked.

Remove the bay leaf and serve with white rice.

TWENTY-THREE
The Sacrament of
the Eucharist

CONTEMPLATE

At the Last Supper, on the night he was betrayed, our Savior instituted the Eucharistic sacrifice of his Body and Blood. This he did in order to perpetuate the sacrifice of the cross throughout the ages until he should come again, and so to entrust to his beloved Spouse, the Church, a memorial of his death and resurrection: a sacrament of love, a sign of unity, a bond of charity, a Paschal banquet in which Christ is consumed, the mind is filled with grace, and a pledge of future glory is given to us.

—*Sacrosanctum Concilium* 47[22]

PREPARATIONS

Decide in advance if you'll enlist helpers to assist with making dinner and for help with setting the table. If time allows, read the Contemplate passage and think about it during the day. Also, read the Dinner Table Teaching in advance of your dinner time.

OPENING PRAYER
(to be read out loud by parent or guardian or by all)

Dear Lord, Jesus, please visit our family, blessed with one another and with food to eat. Please take care of those who are lacking in food and do not have a family. *Grace Before Meals. Hail Mary.*

DINNER TABLE TEACHING

Read the Contemplate passage and this Dinner
Table Teaching out loud to the family.

The word *eucharist* means thanksgiving. It is a sacrament and a sacrifice. The Eucharist is at the very heart of our faith and worship. Jesus has given us the gift of Himself! The Church teaches us, "The Eucharist is the heart and the summit of the Church's life, for in it Christ associates his Church and all her members with his sacrifice of praise and thanksgiving offered once for all on the cross to his Father; by this sacrifice he pours out the graces of salvation on his Body which is the Church" (CCC 1407).

The sacrament of the Eucharist or First Holy Communion is one of the three sacraments of initiation. (The other two are Baptism and Confirmation.) We are heartily prodded by Jesus's words, "I am the living bread that came down out of heaven; if anyone eats of this bread, he will live forever. . . . He who eats My flesh and drinks My blood has eternal life and . . . abides in Me, and I in him" (John 6:51, 54, 56 NASB).

Jesus gave His priests the role to change bread and wine into his body and blood at the Last Supper when he said: "Do this in remembrance of me" (Lk. 2:19). The priest utters the words of consecration, but Christ Himself through the action of the Holy Spirit does the transforming (CCC 1105). The Church uses the words, *really, truly,* and *substantially* to explain Christ's whole and true presence in the Holy Eucharist. The doctrine of the Holy Eucharist contains many mysteries that are difficult to explain and understand. But Catholics believe Christ's words: "This is My body. . . . This is My blood."

The Eucharist gives us much strength for the daily journey of our lives.

REFLECTION QUESTIONS

Ask the children to share their thoughts.

Why is the Eucharist so important?

What does *eucharist* mean?

Who gave the gift of the Eucharist to the Church?

Can the Eucharist help you? List two ways or share an experience.

CLOSING PRAYER

(to pray together out loud)

Grace After Meals. Blessed Mother, Mary, please be with me when I receive the Eucharist and help me to grow in holiness. Please pray for us. *Our Father.*

Look over the optional activities below and discuss with the family to see if you can carry them out during the upcoming week.

WEEKDAY PRAYER

Each day of the upcoming week at the dinner table, pray this simple prayer.

Dear Lord, Jesus, open my heart to Your love. Help me to understand more about the depth of Your love for me. Amen.

THEME EXTENSION

This activity is for anyone in the family.

Think about Christ's words: "This is My body. . . . This is My blood." Take time to thank God for the great gift of the Eucharist.

EXTRA CREDIT!

This activity is for anyone in the family.

Sometime this week, take a few moments to do a surprise work of mercy for someone in your family.

TWENTY-FOUR
The Sacrament of Penance

CONTEMPLATE

The forgiveness of sins committed after Baptism is conferred
by a particular sacrament called the sacrament of conversion,
confession, penance, or reconciliation.

—CCC 1486

PREPARATIONS

*Decide in advance if you'll enlist helpers to assist with making dinner and
for help with setting the table. If time allows, read the Contemplate passage and
think about it during the day. Also, read the Dinner Table Teaching in advance
of your dinner time.*

OPENING PRAYER
(to be read out loud by parent or guardian or by all)

Dear Lord, Jesus, please visit our family, blessed with one another and
with food to eat. Please take care of those who are lacking in food and do
not have a family. *Grace Before Meals. Hail Mary.*

DINNER TABLE TEACHING
*Read the Contemplate passage and this Dinner
Table Teaching out loud to the family.*

Our hearts are heavy when we are in sin. Sin is an offense against God. And it damages our communion with the Church, too. When we go through the sacrament of Confession or Penance with a contrite heart, we are forgiven by God *and* reconciled with the Church.

Our merciful Jesus is constantly calling all of us to an interior conversion of heart. He wants us to repent of our sins and start anew. We confess our sins in the sacrament of Confession. Then, the Church teaches, there is more: "Raised up from sin, the sinner must still recover his full spiritual health by doing something more to make amends for the sin: he must 'make satisfaction for' or 'expiate' his sins. This satisfaction is also called 'penance'" (CCC 1459).

Each day we can work out our salvation and come closer to Jesus: "Conversion is accomplished in daily life by gestures of reconciliation, concern for the poor, the exercise and defense of justice and right, by the admission of faults to one's brethren, fraternal correction, revision of life, examination of conscience, spiritual direction, acceptance of suffering, endurance of persecution for the sake of righteousness. Taking up one's cross each day and following Jesus is the surest way of penance" (CCC 1435).

The *Catechism* also tells us:

The spiritual effects of the sacrament of Penance are:

- reconciliation with God by which the penitent recovers grace;
- reconciliation with the Church;
- remission of the eternal punishment incurred by mortal sins;
- remission, at least in part, of temporal punishments resulting from sin;
- peace and serenity of conscience, and spiritual consolation;
- an increase of spiritual strength for the Christian battle. (CCC 1496)

REFLECTION QUESTIONS
Ask the children to share their thoughts.

Why should you go to Confession?

What are some ways that you can show mercy and forgiveness to your family members?

How can you ask forgiveness of someone?

What are some of the spiritual effects of going to Confession?

CLOSING PRAYER
(to pray together out loud)

Grace After Meals. Blessed Mother, Mary, please pray for us and help us to be more forgiving and also to ask forgiveness of others. *Our Father.*

———

Look over the optional activities below and discuss with the family to see if you can carry them out during the upcoming week.

WEEKDAY PRAYER
Each day of the upcoming week at the dinner table, pray this simple prayer.

Dear Lord, Jesus, open my heart to Your love. Forgive me of my sins. Amen.

Also, pray this prayer:

Act of Contrition

O my God,

I am heartily sorry for

having offended Thee,

and I detest all my sins,

because I dread the loss of heaven,

and the pains of hell;

but most of all because

they offend Thee, my God,

Who are all good and

deserving of all my love.

I firmly resolve,

with the help of Thy grace,

to confess my sins,

to do penance,

and to amend my life.

Amen.

THEME EXTENSION
This activity is for anyone in the family.

Make a point of forgiving someone who has hurt you even when he or she hasn't asked for forgiveness. You can do this silently as you pray for him or her. Or, you can speak to the person about it if you feel it would be appropriate to do so.

EXTRA CREDIT!
This activity is for the entire family.

Sometime this week, take a few moments to schedule a time to bring the family to Confession. Do your best not to put this off.

TWENTY-FIVE

The Sacrament of the Anointing of the Sick

CONTEMPLATE

"By the sacred anointing of the sick and the prayer of the priests the whole Church commends those who are ill to the suffering and glorified Lord, that he may raise them up and save them. And indeed she exhorts them to contribute to the good of the People of God by freely uniting themselves to the Passion and death of Christ."

—*Lumen Gentium* 11[23]

PREPARATIONS

Decide in advance if you'll enlist helpers to assist with making dinner and for help with setting the table. If time allows, read the Contemplate passage and think about it during the day. Also, read the Dinner Table Teaching in advance of your dinner time.

OPENING PRAYER

(to be read out loud by parent or guardian or by all)

Dear Lord, Jesus, please visit our family, blessed with one another and with food to eat. Please take care of those who are lacking in food and do not have a family. *Grace Before Meals. Hail Mary.*

DINNER TABLE TEACHING

Read the Contemplate passage and this Dinner
Table Teaching out loud to the family.

"Is any among you sick? Let him call for the elders of the Church, and let them pray over him, anointing him with oil in the name of the Lord; and the prayer of faith will save the sick man, and the Lord will raise him up; and if he has committed sins, he will be forgiven" (Jas. 5:14–15).

Illness can cause you to become self-absorbed or angry with God. It can also cause you to turn to God for help, knowing your own limitations. We learn through the Scriptures that Jesus was compassionate toward the sick and often healed them. "In the sacraments Christ continues to 'touch' us in order to heal us" (CCC 1504).

Special grace is imparted to a person receiving the beautiful transforming sacrament of Anointing of the Sick. The *Catechism* tells us:

The special grace of the sacrament of the Anointing of the Sick has as its effects:

- the uniting of the sick person to the passion of Christ, for his own good and that of the whole Church;
- the strengthening, peace, and courage to endure in a Christian manner the sufferings of illness or old age;
- the forgiveness of sins, if the sick person was not able to obtain it through the sacrament of Penance;
- the restoration of health, if it is conducive to the salvation of his soul;
- the preparation for passing over to eternal life. (CCC 1532)

Years ago, the anointing of the sick was called "Extreme Unction" and was administered only when someone was dying. Today, the anointing of the sick is given not only to those who are dying, but also to the sick who are not in any danger of dying.

I have received this sacrament a number of times already in my own life.

Each time it has brought many blessings. I vividly remember the distinct lovely aroma of the holy oils, which I smelled as the priest anointed my forehead and hands. It lingered for some time afterward.

When anointing the sick, the priest says, "Through this holy anointing may the Lord in his love and mercy help you with the grace of the Holy Spirit. May the Lord who frees you from sin save you and raise you up" (CCC 1513).

REFLECTION QUESTIONS
Ask the children to share their thoughts.

Why should we call a priest when someone is seriously ill?

What can the Anointing of the Sick do for us if we are very sick?

What can the sacrament do for someone who is at the point of death?

CLOSING PRAYER
(to pray together out loud)

Grace After Meals. Blessed Mother, Mary, pray for us and guide us so that one day we will be with you in heaven. *Our Father.*

Look over the optional activities below and discuss with the family to see if you can carry them out during the upcoming week.

WEEKDAY PRAYER
Each day of the upcoming week at the dinner table, pray this simple prayer.

Dear Lord, Jesus, open my heart to Your love. Help me to be more attentive to the sick and suffering. Amen.

THEME EXTENSION

This activity is for anyone in the family, or it can be carried out together.

Call a relative or friend who is sick or elderly. They will surely be happy to hear from you!

EXTRA CREDIT!

This activity is for parents or guardians.

Sometime this week, take a few moments to get in touch with an older relative and ask if he or she would be willing to share a favorite recipe. Write it down, and be sure to note your relative's name with the recipe. Endeavor to make the recipe and enjoy it with your family soon.

TWENTY-SIX
The Sacrament
of Holy Orders

CONTEMPLATE

Holy Orders is the sacrament through which the mission
entrusted by Christ to his apostles continues to be exercised
in the Church until the end of time: thus it is the sacrament
of apostolic ministry. It includes three degrees: episcopate,
presbyterate, and diaconate.

—CCC 1536

PREPARATIONS

*Decide in advance if you'll enlist helpers to assist with making dinner and
for help with setting the table. If time allows, read the Contemplate passage and
think about it during the day. Also, read the Dinner Table Teaching in advance
of your dinner time.*

OPENING PRAYER
(to be read out loud by parent or guardian or by all)

Dear Lord, Jesus, please visit our family, blessed with one another and
with food to eat. Please take care of those who are lacking in food and do
not have a family. *Grace Before Meals. Hail Mary.*

DINNER TABLE TEACHING

Read the Contemplate passage and this Dinner
Table Teaching out loud to the family.

The Church teaches: "The whole Church is a priestly people. Through Baptism all the faithful share in the priesthood of Christ. This participation is called the 'common priesthood of the faithful'" (CCC 1591). Some are called to another priestly mission of Christ, the important ministry bestowed through the sacrament of Holy Orders upon suitable baptized men. Holy Orders is a special and important sacrament. For the ministerial priesthood, "the task is to serve in the name and in the person of Christ the Head in the midst of the community" (CCC 1591).

There are three degrees of the sacrament: two ministerial—bishop and priest—and the deacon, "intended to help and serve them" (CCC 1554). Through the ministerial priesthood Christ continuously guides, builds up, and ministers to his Church.

As with Baptism and Confirmation, the sacrament of Holy Orders imparts an indelible mark on the person's soul (see CCC 1583).

When St. John Paul II was a little boy, his devout mother constructed a small altar in his bedroom. This inspired young Karol Józef to play act as a priest offering many "Masses" on his little altar. Many years later, he was ordained a priest. Later on, he became a bishop, then an archbishop, a cardinal, and finally a pope. It would seem that this mother's efforts to inspire the young Karol Józef fostered the vocation in his heart.

REFLECTION QUESTIONS

Ask the children to share their thoughts.

How many degrees are there in the sacrament of Holy Orders?

Do you realize that "The ministerial priesthood has the task not only of representing Christ—Head of the Church—before the assembly of the faithful, but also of acting in the name of the whole Church when presenting to God the prayer of the Church, and above all when offering the Eucharistic sacrifice"? (CCC 1552)

Because Holy Orders is such an important job, it would seem important to pray for all priests and bishops as well as deacons. Do you pray for them? Will you?

CLOSING PRAYER
(to pray together out loud)

Grace After Meals. Blessed Mother, Mary, please pray for us. *Our Father.*

Look over the optional activities below and discuss with the family to see if you can carry them out during the upcoming week.

WEEKDAY PRAYER
Each day of the upcoming week at the dinner table, pray this simple prayer.

Dear Lord, Jesus, open my heart to Your love. St. John Paul II, please pray for me. Amen.

THEME EXTENSION
This activity is for anyone in the family, or it can be carried out together.

Pray each day for priests, bishops, and deacons, as well as for the Holy Father, the pope.

EXTRA CREDIT!

This activity is the entire family.

Sometime this week, take a few moments to make a homemade greeting card for the priest, or each priest, at your parish. If possible, also make a special dessert or batch of cookies. You can double the batch and enjoy the dessert yourselves sometime this week. When you go to Mass, hand deliver the gift of the dessert and the card or cards to express your appreciation for each of your priests' loving and dedicated service.

• RECIPE •

Taco Soup

My friend Gail Buckley shares one of her favorite recipes. She explains: "This soup is not only delicious and the perfect meal for a cold wintry day, but it seems almost *miraculous.*" One snowy day Gail was craving this soup, so she checked to see if she had all the ingredients in the house. She was snowed in and could not go to the store. Gail was happy to find everything except enough ground beef—the recipe called for more than twice what she had on hand. "But I was determined, so I made it with just the little bit of meat I had and it turned out great. The 'miraculous' thing is that every spoonful of that soup was full of meat right down to the bottom of the pot. So, if you don't have two pounds of ground beef, don't be discouraged— make it anyway!"

Gail believes "this soup is delicious, easy to make, great for large families or groups, and economical. It makes a large amount, and when it starts getting low, all you have to do is add some more beans or corn to stretch it. And best of all, you can freeze it and have it again and again. All you need to do is add rolls or cornbread and you have a delicious and filling meal."

Ingredients

- 2 lbs. ground beef (or substitute with ground chicken or turkey)
- 1 medium onion, chopped
- 3 cans stewed tomatoes, undrained (Gail recommends "petite, chopped")
- 1 16-oz. can kidney beans, undrained
- 1 16-oz. can chili beans, undrained
- 1 can yellow or white hominy (or yellow corn), *drained*
- 1½ cups water
- 1 package taco seasoning
- ½ tsp. salt
- ½ tsp. pepper

Directions

In a large pot, cook the ground beef (or ground chicken or turkey) and onions together until brown. You can salt and pepper the meat while it is cooking. Add taco seasoning to meat and onions, and stir together. Then add all other ingredients, stirring until hot. Enjoy!

Gail's tip: "I think this soup is perfectly seasoned; however, on occasion I've added too much taco seasoning when stretching it, which made it saltier and spicier. Adding 1–2 tablespoons of sugar and a cup of water will usually fix this problem."

TWENTY-SEVEN
The Sacrament
of Matrimony

CONTEMPLATE

The matrimonial covenant, by which a man and a woman establish between themselves a partnership of the whole of life, is by its nature ordered toward the good of the spouses and the procreation and education of offspring; this covenant between baptized persons has been raised by Christ the Lord to the dignity of a sacrament.

—CCC 1601

PREPARATIONS

Decide in advance if you'll enlist helpers to assist with making dinner and for help with setting the table. If time allows, read the Contemplate passage and think about it during the day. Also, read the Dinner Table Teaching in advance of your dinner time.

OPENING PRAYER
(to be read out loud by parent or guardian or by all)

Dear Lord, Jesus, please visit our family, blessed with one another and with food to eat. Please take care of those who are lacking in food and do not have a family. *Grace Before Meals. Hail Mary.*

DINNER TABLE TEACHING

Read the Contemplate passage and this Dinner
Table Teaching out loud to the family.

God has created man and woman. Scripture tells us that man and woman were made for each other. God has created a special partnership for them called matrimony or marriage. Marriage between a baptized man and woman is sacred, and its purpose is for the good of one another and the procreation of children. Through prayer, the couple can call upon the graces of the sacrament for the strength and courage to continue serving one another through thick and thin as they stay faithful to their wedding vows.

Much grace is bestowed upon the couple within this special sacrament, which mirrors the love of Christ and His Church. "The sacrament of Matrimony signifies the union of Christ and the Church. It gives spouses the grace to love each other with the love with which Christ has loved his Church; the grace of the sacrament thus perfects the human love of the spouses, strengthens their indissoluble unity, and sanctifies them on the way to eternal life" (CCC 1661).

A lot happens within the walls of a Christian home—more than meets the eye. Husband and wife help one another to get to heaven through their sacrificial giving. Parents teach their children the faith and how to live virtuously through the give-and-take of daily life. The Church instructs parents to be sure to be the first and foremost educators of the faith to their children. "The Christian home is the place where children receive the first proclamation of the faith. For this reason the family home is rightly called 'the domestic church,' a community of grace and prayer, a school of human virtues and of Christian charity" (CCC 1666).

Spouses help to work out one another's sanctification through praying for one another, living out the virtues, and practicing continual tenderness and forgiveness within the heart of the home.

REFLECTION QUESTIONS

Ask the children to share their thoughts.

Why are families important?

What two people does a family start with?

How can husband and wife help one another to get to heaven? List three ways.

CLOSING PRAYER

(to pray together out loud)

Grace After Meals. Sts. Zélie and Louis Martin (parents of St. Thérèse of Lisieux), please pray for us. *Our Father.*

Look over the optional activities below and discuss with the family to see if you can carry them out during the upcoming week.

WEEKDAY PRAYER

Each day of the upcoming week at the dinner table, pray this simple prayer.

Dear Lord, Jesus, open my heart to Your love. Sts. Zélie and Louis Martin, teach us to love one another in our family. Amen.

THEME EXTENSION

This activity is for anyone in the family.

If you experience a difficulty or doubt, turn to Sts. Zélie and Louis Martin, asking them to intercede for you and help you to practice the heroic virtues.

EXTRA CREDIT!

This activity is for anyone in the family.

Sometime this week, take a few moments to research Sts. Zélie and Louis Martin. Share the information that you found at the dinner table one evening.

TWENTY-EIGHT
About the First Commandment

CONTEMPLATE

I am the Lord your God: you shall not have strange Gods before me.
—First Commandment[24]

PREPARATIONS

Decide in advance if you'll enlist helpers to assist with making dinner and for help with setting the table. If time allows, read the Contemplate passage and think about it during the day. Also, read the Dinner Table Teaching in advance of your dinner time.

OPENING PRAYER
(to be read out loud by parent or guardian or by all)

Dear Lord, Jesus, please visit our family, blessed with one another and with food to eat. Please take care of those who are lacking in food and do not have a family. *Grace Before Meals. Hail Mary.*

DINNER TABLE TEACHING
*Read the Contemplate passage and this Dinner
Table Teaching out loud to the family.*

The first of the Ten Commandments tells us that we are to love and worship God alone. And we are to do it with everything we have. In other words, nothing comes before God. We are to love him and hope in him above anything else. The Church teaches:

> The first commandment embraces faith, hope, and charity. When we say "God" we confess a constant, unchangeable being, always the same, faithful and just, without any evil. It follows that we must necessarily accept his words and have complete faith in him and acknowledge his authority. He is almighty, merciful, and infinitely beneficent. Who could not place all hope in him? Who could not love him when contemplating the treasures of goodness and love he has poured out on us? Hence the formula God employs in the Scripture at the beginning and end of his commandments: "I am the Lord" (CCC 2086).

We live in a fast-paced world, which beckons for our attention in myriad ways at every moment. We must be sure to form a firm foundation of prayer so that we are ever mindful of God in our lives and so that we can receive the graces from him that we need to combat the false charms of a darkened culture. If we are not careful and prayerful, we could end up worshiping a "strange God" that we create out of some interest or thing. Placing an inordinate amount of attention on anything can get us into trouble and draw us away from the one true God who deserves our love and attention.

REFLECTION QUESTIONS
Ask the children to share their thoughts.

What can you do to show God you love him? List three ways.

What is a "strange god"?

Why is it important to pray?

How can you keep from falling into the temptation of putting too much emphasis on things rather than God?

CLOSING PRAYER
(to pray together out loud)

Grace After Meals. Blessed Mother, Mary, please pray for us. *Our Father.*

———

Look over the optional activities below and discuss with the family to see if you can carry them out during the upcoming week.

WEEKDAY PRAYER
Each day of the upcoming week at the dinner table, pray this simple prayer.

Dear Lord, Jesus, open my heart to Your love. All of the angels and saints, please pray for me. Amen.

THEME EXTENSION
This activity is for anyone in the family, or it can be carried out together.

The Church teaches, "To adore God is to acknowledge, in respect and absolute submission, the 'nothingness of the creature' who would not exist but for God. To adore God is to praise and exalt him and to humble oneself, as Mary did in the Magnificat, confessing with gratitude that he has done great things and holy is his name. The worship of the one God sets man free from turning in on himself, from the slavery of sin and the idolatry of the world" (CCC 2097).

During the upcoming week, find some quiet time to be alone with God and to adore him.

EXTRA CREDIT!

This activity is for anyone in the family.

Sometime this week, take a few moments to plan on unplugging from technology, as a family or individually—for an hour, or maybe a day. During that period, instead of being connected to technology, do some spiritual reading as a family or alone.

TWENTY-NINE
About the Second Commandment

CONTEMPLATE

You shall not take the name of the Lord your God in vain.

—Second Commandment

PREPARATIONS

Decide in advance if you'll enlist helpers to assist with making dinner and for help with setting the table. If time allows, read the Contemplate passage and think about it during the day. Also, read the Dinner Table Teaching in advance of your dinner time.

OPENING PRAYER
(to be read out loud by parent or guardian or by all)

Dear Lord, Jesus, please visit our family, blessed with one another and with food to eat. Please take care of those who are lacking in food and do not have a family. *Grace Before Meals. Hail Mary.*

DINNER TABLE TEACHING
Read the Contemplate passage and this Dinner Table Teaching out loud to the family.

We read in the Psalms, "O Lord, our Lord, how majestic is thy name in all the earth!" (Ps. 8:1). Our Lord's name is holy and deserving of respect. But people can be very lax and even disrespectful in their speech. Many use the Lord's name in vain countless times per day. It is very common to say, "Oh my God!" But is this pleasing to God?

The Church teaches, "The second commandment *prescribes respect for the Lord's name*. Like the first commandment, it belongs to the virtue of religion and more particularly it governs our use of speech in sacred matters" (CCC 2142). The second commandment also forbids false oaths.

One time when out at a public place a woman I knew exclaimed to me, "Jesus Christ, Donna! Congratulations on your new book!" I was a bit shocked, immediately blessing myself with the Sign of the Cross right in front of her in reverence to Jesus, whose name was being used in vain. Perhaps my earnest gesture touched the woman in some way, I don't know, but I felt a need to make up for the carelessness and insensitivity of the woman. We must be careful with our speech so as not to offend God and also to set a good example to others.

REFLECTION QUESTIONS
Ask the children to share their thoughts.

How can you keep from using the Lord's name in vain?

What can you do if someone uses the Lord's name in vain in your presence?

How can you show God that you love him?

CLOSING PRAYER

(to pray together out loud)

Grace After Meals. Blessed Mother, Mary, please pray for us. *Our Father.*

———

Look over the optional activities below and discuss with the family to see if you can carry them out during the upcoming week.

WEEKDAY PRAYER

Each day of the upcoming week at the dinner table, pray this simple prayer.

Dear Lord, Jesus, open my heart to Your love. Help me never to take Your name in vain. Amen.

THEME EXTENSION

This activity is for anyone in the family, or to can be carried out together.

Read about what Jesus says during the Sermon on the Mount in Matthew 5:33–37.

EXTRA CREDIT!

This activity is for anyone in the family.

Sometime this week, take a few moments to reflect on the holiness of God's name. Perhaps you can research saints who proclaimed the sacredness of God's name. Share what you learn at the dinner table one evening.

———

THIRTY
About the Third Commandment

CONTEMPLATE

Remember to keep holy the Lord's Day.

—Third Commandment

PREPARATIONS

Decide in advance if you'll enlist helpers to assist with making dinner and for help with setting the table. If time allows, read the Contemplate passage and think about it during the day. Also, read the Dinner Table Teaching in advance of your dinner time.

OPENING PRAYER

(to be read out loud by parent or guardian or by all)

Dear Lord, Jesus, please visit our family, blessed with one another and with food to eat. Please take care of those who are lacking in food and do not have a family. *Grace Before Meals. Hail Mary.*

DINNER TABLE TEACHING

Read the Contemplate passage and this Dinner Table Teaching out loud to the family.

On a Sunday morning, shopping-mall parking lots are much more full than church parking lots. Have we forgotten to keep the Lord's Day holy? Do we care? The Psalms proclaim, "This is the day which the Lord has made; let us rejoice and be glad in it" (Ps. 118:24).

Christ's resurrection is celebrated by the Church on Sundays, and we are expected to keep the day holy with prayer and participation at holy Mass. The Church teaches: "On Sundays and other holy days of obligation the faithful are bound to participate in the Mass" (*Code of Canon Law* 1247).

St. John Chrysostom expressed the benefits of praying in community at Mass when he said, "You cannot pray at home as at church, where there is a great multitude, where exclamations are cried out to God as from one great heart, and where there is something more: the union of minds, the accord of souls, the bond of charity, the prayers of the priests" (CCC 2179).

In addition, Sundays are meant as a day of rest from work and excessive activity. "On Sundays and other holy days of obligation the faithful are bound . . . to abstain from those labors and business concerns which impede the worship to be rendered to God, the joy which is proper to the Lord's Day, or the proper relaxation of mind and body" (*Code of Canon Law* 1247). We should plan so that we don't end up needing to spend time shopping on Sundays. If we make a point to rest and keep Sundays holy, our spirits will be wonderfully refreshed.

REFLECTION QUESTIONS

Ask the children to share their thoughts.

Why is it essential to keep Sundays and holy days of obligation holy?

How can you observe the holiness of Sundays? List three ways.

List three ways in which we could displease God on Sundays.

Can you be an example to others in keeping the Lord's Day holy?

CLOSING PRAYER
(to pray together out loud)

Grace After Meals. St. John Chrysostom, please pray for us. *Our Father.*

———

Look over the optional activities below and discuss with the family to see if you can carry them out during the upcoming week.

WEEKDAY PRAYER
Each day of the upcoming week at the dinner table, pray this simple prayer.

Dear Lord, Jesus, open my heart to Your love. I love You and want to keep Your day holy. Amen.

THEME EXTENSION
This activity is for the entire family.

Think about how you plan to spend your upcoming Sunday—this might include being in touch with relatives, studying your faith through spiritual reading, playing a board game with your family, taking time to rest, and possibly unplugging from technology.

EXTRA CREDIT!
This activity is for anyone in the family.

Sometime this week, take a few moments to plan a special outing or activity that your family can enjoy on an upcoming Sunday—something that can enrich your faith and give rest to your mind. It could be a mini-retreat, or a pilgrimage to a local holy place.

• RECIPE •

Chicken and Sausage Gumbo

My friend Lisa Andrus shares her gumbo recipe. Lisa lives in south Louisiana, and gumbo is a tradition in Lisa's family. I have had the pleasure and blessing of eating at Lisa's table when visiting her parish to give talks.

Lisa grew up eating gumbo, as did her parents, but she didn't learn to make a roux until after many years of cooking. "I watched others make it and tried and failed." Lisa recounted exuberantly the time she made her very first roux successfully: "My son, Dwight, actually taught me how to make a roux after being taught by his grandfather—my father-in-law . . . definitely the best cook in our family. One time I was in Georgia visiting my daughter and wanted to make a gumbo. I called my son and he coached me over the phone and I actually did it!"

Lisa feels the urge to make gumbo when it starts to get chilly. "Gumbo is comforting and delicious, perfect for a cold night or just a gathering with friends, as it serves a lot of people." There are many variations. People use different amounts of flour and stock. Most add filé—powdered sassafras leaves—which acts as a thickener. Using less rice makes a much lighter meal. "But all gumbo is delicious and is the ultimate comfort food," Lisa says.

An interesting side note: Lisa's ninety-two-year-old mother, Vita (whose father was in World War I), says they did not eat a lot of soup and gumbo. Her husband was a Louisiana farmer who needed something more substantial after working outdoors on the farm all day. Lisa adds, "I can see how my grandfather would have needed to eat meat and potatoes—actually in Louisiana it would have been rice—after a hard day's work." And, her mother reminds her, they ate a lot of sweet potatoes.

Ingredients

- 1 cup all-purpose flour
- 1 cup vegetable oil
- 1 large onion, chopped
- 1 cup celery, chopped (about 2 stalks)
- 1 cup green bell pepper, chopped
- 3 quarts chicken stock
- 1 5-lb. chicken, cut into pieces
- 1 pound smoked pork sausage, sliced
- salt and pepper
- garlic powder
- ½ cup green onions, chopped

Directions

Make a roux in a heavy pot using flour and oil, stirring constantly until the mixture is a dark rust color or dark brown (depending on how one likes it), being careful not to let it burn. Reduce heat and stir in all the cut vegetables, except green onions, and continue cooking. Heat chicken stock separately, and then slowly stir into the roux and vegetables. Add chicken and sausage and all other ingredients, except green onions, and simmer slowly until chicken is cooked, stirring frequently, about 1½ hours. Season to taste. Add green onions just before serving. Serve in soup bowls over cooked rice. It is common to serve potato salad and garlic bread alongside the gumbo. Enjoy!

THIRTY-ONE
About the Fourth Commandment

CONTEMPLATE

Honor your father and your mother.

—Fourth Commandment

PREPARATIONS

Decide in advance if you'll enlist helpers to assist with making dinner and for help with setting the table. If time allows, read the Contemplate passage and think about it during the day. Also, read the Dinner Table Teaching in advance of your dinner time.

OPENING PRAYER
(to be read out loud by parent or guardian or by all)

Dear Lord, Jesus, please visit our family, blessed with one another and with food to eat. Please take care of those who are lacking in food and do not have a family. *Grace Before Meals. Hail Mary.*

DINNER TABLE TEACHING
Read the Contemplate passage and this Dinner Table Teaching out loud to the family.

The fourth commandment focuses on the relationship of a child to his or her father and mother. The Church teaches that this is "because this relationship is the most universal. It likewise concerns the ties of kinship between members of the extended family. It requires honor, affection, and gratitude toward elders and ancestors. Finally, it extends to the duties of pupils to teachers, employees to employers, subordinates to leaders, citizens to their country, and to those who administer or govern it" (CCC 2199).

In a day when it seems there is much disrespect in our world, it is even more important to teach children to respect their parents and those in authority, provided the authority is not contrary to the demands of moral law. "According to the fourth commandment, God has willed that, after him, we should honor our parents and those whom he has vested with authority for our good" (CCC 2248).

REFLECTION QUESTIONS

Ask the children to share their thoughts.

What are some ways that parents can be honored by their children?
List three ways in which the culture does not support family life.
What can you do to support family life?

CLOSING PRAYER
(to pray together out loud)

Grace After Meals. Holy Family of Nazareth, please pray for us. *Our Father.*

Look over the optional activities below and discuss with the family to see if you can carry them out during the upcoming week.

WEEKDAY PRAYER

Each day of the upcoming week at the dinner table, pray this simple prayer.

Dear Lord, Jesus, open my heart to Your love. Holy Family of Nazareth, teach me to show honor and respect to parents and those in authority. Amen.

THEME EXTENSION

This activity is for anyone in the family, or it can be carried out together.

Take some time unplugged from technology—instead, get involved with the family by having fun, perhaps by playing a board game or having a heartfelt discussion reminiscing about family history.

EXTRA CREDIT!

This activity is for anyone in the family.

Sometime this week, take a few moments to reach out to older relatives, asking if they could share a favorite recipe for you to write down and add to your recipe box or notebook. Be sure to include your relative's name. If possible, visit with your relative very soon.

THIRTY-TWO
About the Fifth Commandment

CONTEMPLATE

You shall not kill.

—Fifth Commandment

PREPARATIONS

Decide in advance if you'll enlist helpers to assist with making dinner and for help with setting the table. If time allows, read the Contemplate passage and think about it during the day. Also, read the Dinner Table Teaching in advance of your dinner time.

OPENING PRAYER
(to be read out loud by parent or guardian or by all)

Dear Lord, Jesus, please visit our family, blessed with one another and with food to eat. Please take care of those who are lacking in food and do not have a family. *Grace Before Meals. Hail Mary.*

DINNER TABLE TEACHING
Read the Contemplate passage and this Dinner Table Teaching out loud to the family.

The taking of human life is a very grave sin. War should be avoided whenever possible. Suicide is forbidden by the fifth commandment. Euthanasia is considered to be murder even though some attempt to justify it as a merciful act. The Church teaches, "*Human life is sacred* because from its beginning it involves the creative action of God and it remains forever in a special relationship with the Creator, who is its sole end. God alone is the Lord of life from its beginning until its end: no one can under any circumstance claim for himself the right directly to destroy an innocent human being."[25]

Sadly, countless human lives have been taken through the act of abortion. The Church teaches, "Since the first century the Church has affirmed the moral evil of every procured abortion. This teaching has not changed and remains unchangeable. Direct abortion, that is to say, abortion willed either as an end or a means, is gravely contrary to the moral law" (CCC 2271).

Mother Teresa did not mince words about the sin of abortion as she spoke at the 1994 National Prayer Breakfast in Washington, DC: "By abortion, the mother does not learn to love, but kills even her own child to solve her problems. And, by abortion, that father is told that he does not have to take any responsibility at all for the child he has brought into the world. The father is likely to put other women into the same trouble. So abortion just leads to more abortion. Any country that accepts abortion is not teaching its people to love, but to use any violence to get what they want. This is why the greatest destroyer of love and peace is abortion."[26]

REFLECTION QUESTIONS

Ask the children to share their thoughts.

Why is human life sacred?

What can you do to help raise awareness about the sanctity and dignity of all human life?

How might you be an example to others about the sanctity and dignity of every human life?

CLOSING PRAYER
(to pray together out loud)

Grace After Meals. St. Teresa of Calcutta, please pray for us. All of the angels and saints, please pray for us. *Our Father.*

———

Look over the optional activities below and discuss with the family to see if you can carry them out during the upcoming week.

WEEKDAY PRAYER
Each day of the upcoming week at the dinner table, pray this simple prayer.

Dear Lord, Jesus, open my heart to Your love. Blessed Mother, Mary, show me how to protect human life. Amen.

Pray the following prayer this week when you are able:

Prayer for the Unborn by Pope Benedict XVI[27]

Lord Jesus, You who faithfully visit and fulfill with your Presence the Church and the history of men; You who in the miraculous Sacrament of your Body and Blood render us participants in divine Life and allow us a foretaste of the joy of eternal Life; We adore and bless you.

Prostrated before You, source and lover of Life, truly present and alive among us, we beg you.

Reawaken in us respect for every unborn life, make us capable of seeing in the fruit of the maternal womb the miraculous work of the Creator, open our hearts to generously welcoming every child that comes into life.

Bless all families, sanctify the union of spouses, render fruitful their love.

Accompany the choices of legislative assemblies with the light of your Spirit, so that peoples and nations may recognize and respect the sacred nature of life, of every human life.

Guide the work of scientists and doctors, so that all progress contributes to the integral well-being of the person, and no one endures suppression or injustice.

Give creative charity to administrators and economists, so they may realize and promote sufficient conditions so that young families can serenely embrace the birth of new children.

Console the married couples who suffer because they are unable to have children and in Your goodness provide for them.

Teach us all to care for orphaned or abandoned children, so they may experience the warmth of your Charity, the consolation of your divine Heart.

Together with Mary, Your Mother, the great believer, in whose womb you took on our human nature, we wait to receive from You, our Only True Good and Savior, the strength to love and serve life, in anticipation of living forever in You, in communion with the Blessed Trinity.

THEME EXTENSION
This activity is for anyone in the family.

Fast or make a sacrifice in some way and offer it to God for the unborn and elderly in danger of death.

EXTRA CREDIT!

This activity is for anyone in the family.

Sometime this week, take a few moments to write a poem as a family in honor of human life and send it to your local newspaper for the "Letters to the Editor" section.

THIRTY-THREE
About the Sixth Commandment

CONTEMPLATE

You shall not commit adultery.

—Sixth Commandment

PREPARATIONS

Decide in advance if you'll enlist helpers to assist with making dinner and for help with setting the table. If time allows, read the Contemplate passage and think about it during the day. Also, read the Dinner Table Teaching in advance of your dinner time.

Today's teaching might be considered a delicate matter, so proceed in the way that is appropriate for your family.

OPENING PRAYER

(to be read out loud by parent or guardian or by all)

Dear Lord, Jesus, please visit our family, blessed with one another and with food to eat. Please take care of those who are lacking in food and do not have a family. *Grace Before Meals. Hail Mary.*

DINNER TABLE TEACHING
*Read the Contemplate passage and this Dinner
Table Teaching out loud to the family.*

Every baptized Christian is called to a life of chastity according to his or her walk of life. This includes "an apprenticeship in self-mastery" (CCC 2395).

"Chastity is a moral virtue. It is also a gift from God, a *grace*, a fruit of spiritual effort" (2345). A married man and woman lovingly and chastely commit to one another for life through the sacrament of their marriage vows. It is a sin against the sixth commandment for the married man or woman to have inappropriate relations with others.

The *Catechism* notes: "St. John Chrysostom suggests that young husbands should say to their wives: I have taken you in my arms, and I love you, and I prefer you to my life itself. For the present life is nothing, and my most ardent dream is to spend it with you in such a way that we may be assured of not being separated in the life reserved for us. . . . I place your love above all things, and nothing would be more bitter or painful to me than to be of a different mind than you" (CCC 2365).

To sin against the sixth commandment means to be involved with marital infidelity. "Christ condemns even adultery of mere desire. The sixth commandment and the New Testament forbid adultery absolutely. The prophets denounce the gravity of adultery; they see it as an image of the sin of idolatry" (CCC 2380).

There are other sins against this commandment, which can be usefully explored in the *Catechism* paragraphs 2331–2400.

REFLECTION QUESTIONS

Ask the children to share their thoughts.

Why is it important for a husband and wife to remain faithful to one another?

How can a husband and wife work on their marriage? Will prayer help?

Why is it important not to get caught up in the dark messages of the world?

How can the youth better prepare for marriage?

CLOSING PRAYER

(to pray together out loud)

Grace After Meals. Holy Family of Nazareth, please pray for us. *Our Father.*

Look over the optional activities below and discuss with the family to see if you can carry them out during the upcoming week.

WEEKDAY PRAYER

Each day of the upcoming week at the dinner table, pray this simple prayer.

Dear Lord, Jesus, open my heart to Your love. Blessed Mother, Mary, guide me. St. Joseph, strengthen me. Amen.

THEME EXTENSION

This activity is for parents or guardians.

When you are out at the grocery store or watching television, note just how many magazines and commercials undermine the sanctity of marriage.

I have been known to turn a magazine over in the rack to prevent young eyes from seeing what I feel are inappropriate images. I have also made a point to voice my dissatisfaction about certain magazines being sold in a store. What can you do?

EXTRA CREDIT!

This activity is for parents or guardians.

Sometime this week, take a few moments to read the *Catechism* paragraphs 2331–2400 for your own edification as well as to pass along appropriate information to your family.

• RECIPE •

Strawberry Betty

My friend Barb Scholten shares this special dessert recipe. She said she renamed it "Strawberry Joanne," after her eighty-two-year-old friend who introduced the dessert to her. Barb cautions: "This recipe doesn't look like the deliciousness that it is, by just looking at the recipe." She suggests making it "when strawberries are at their best in June, and served warm, with whipped cream is best—it is simply a treat!!"

This dessert is sometimes called Strawberry Platt. Call it what you like, but have fun making it with the family, and enjoy every morsel!

Ingredients

- 1 quart fresh strawberries, washed, hulled, and sliced
- 1/3 cup sugar
- 1 tbsp. cornstarch
- ½ loaf French bread, cut into ½-inch cubes (about 2–3 cups)
- ½ cup (1 stick) butter, melted
- cooking spray

Directions

Preheat oven to 375°F. Coat an 8-inch square baking dish with cooking spray.

In a large bowl, combine strawberries, sugar, and cornstarch; toss to coat. Add bread cubes and melted butter; mix well. Spoon into baking dish.

Bake for 35 to 40 minutes, or until bubbly and bread is golden. Serve warm.

Barb says: "For a totally awesome dessert, serve this with fresh whipped cream made simply by beating 1 cup (½ pint) of heavy cream with 2 to 3 tbsp. confectioner's sugar until stiff peaks form." It is delicious! Enjoy!

THIRTY-FOUR
About the Seventh Commandment

CONTEMPLATE

You shall not steal.

—Seventh Commandment

PREPARATIONS

Decide in advance if you'll enlist helpers to assist with making dinner and for help with setting the table. If time allows, read the Contemplate passage and think about it during the day. Also, read the Dinner Table Teaching in advance of your dinner time.

OPENING PRAYER

(to be read out loud by parent or guardian or by all)

Dear Lord, Jesus, please visit our family, blessed with one another and with food to eat. Please take care of those who are lacking in food and do not have a family. *Grace Before Meals. Hail Mary.*

DINNER TABLE TEACHING

*Read the Contemplate passage and this Dinner
Table Teaching out loud to the family.*

We should not steal. "The seventh commandment forbids unjustly taking or keeping the goods of one's neighbor and wronging him in any way with respect to his goods. It commands justice and charity in the care of earthly goods and the fruits of men's labor. For the sake of the common good, it requires respect for the universal destination of goods and respect for the right to private property. Christian life strives to order this world's goods to God and to fraternal charity" (CCC 2401).

The commandment also calls us to have a religious respect for the integrity of creation, which God has made for us, our neighbors, and generations to come. We must take care of it and not abuse it in any way.

Another way we can fall into sin with regard to this commandment is to fail in caring for our poor brothers and sisters. St. John Chrysostom explained it in this way: "Not to enable the poor to share in our goods is to steal from them and deprive them of life. The goods we possess are not ours, but theirs" (CCC 2446). Clearly, the Church tells us we are to love one another and care for the less fortunate.

REFLECTION QUESTIONS
Ask the children to share their thoughts.

List three ways that one might break this commandment.
How might you be an example of following this commandment?
What can you do to take care of our planet?
How can you share what you have with the poor? List two ways.

CLOSING PRAYER
(to pray together out loud)

Grace After Meals. St. John Chrysostom, please pray for us. *Our Father.*

Look over the optional activities below and discuss with the family to see if you can carry them out during the upcoming week.

WEEKDAY PRAYER
Each day of the upcoming week at the dinner table, pray this simple prayer.

Dear Lord, Jesus, open my heart to Your love. St. John Chrysostom and St. Teresa of Calcutta, show me how to help the poor. Amen.

THEME EXTENSION
This activity is for anyone in the family.

Think about a way that you can be more mindful about taking care of God's creation as well as the less fortunate.

EXTRA CREDIT!
This activity is for anyone in the family.

This week, try hard to be less involved with your devices (phones, tablets, computers—for work or pleasure) so that you don't miss observing the needs of others around you at home or in the neighborhood, community, and workplace. Try your best daily to choose to be more aware of those who need your attention and love.

Let's lift our eyes off our devices and see what is going on around us. God is counting on us!

• R E C I P E •

Barley Soup (Krupnik)

My Polish godmother, Bertha Barosky, shares one of her favorite recipes. Aunt Bertha is my mother's sister. She tells me, "Growing up in a large family, my mother, your grandmother, did the best she could by serving homemade food every day. There were times when we lived off the land. We had a huge garden, which produced fresh vegetables. There were chickens, ducks, and pigs, which also provided many delicious meals for the whole family." The family worked hard on their small farm. Everyone had chores to do to help out.

"When our father, your grandfather, died, we still maintained the gardens and animals. We always had fresh food, bread, and homemade soups. Fortunately, everyone grew up healthy and lived a good life. This recipe was one of the main staples for us. The kitchen was always warm and cozy and full of great aroma," she recalls with a smile.

Ingredients
- 2 quarts of meat stock
- 2 carrots, diced
- 1 stalk of celery, chopped
- 2 potatoes, diced
- sour cream (optional)
- 6 oz. pearl barley
- cup fresh mushrooms
- 4 tbsp. butter
- salt and pepper to taste

Directions

Wash the barley and cover with 1 cup of meat stock. Bring to boiling point and simmer until tender. Add the butter gradually. Separately, boil the vegetables in the remaining stock. Then add the barley mixture to the vegetables, and season with salt and pepper.

Add a few tablespoons of sour cream if desired. Enjoy!

THIRTY-FIVE
About the Eighth Commandment

CONTEMPLATE

You shall not bear false witness against your neighbor.

—Eighth Commandment

PREPARATIONS

Decide in advance if you'll enlist helpers to assist with making dinner and for help with setting the table. If time allows, read the Contemplate passage and think about it during the day. Also, read the Dinner Table Teaching in advance of your dinner time.

OPENING PRAYER

(to be read out loud by parent or guardian or by all)

Dear Lord, Jesus, please visit our family, blessed with one another and with food to eat. Please take care of those who are lacking in food and do not have a family. *Grace Before Meals. Hail Mary.*

DINNER TABLE TEACHING

*Read the Contemplate passage and this Dinner
Table Teaching out loud to the family.*

As Christians, we are called to be truthful at all times. Lying is destructive, and people's private lives deserve to be protected. Combine the two, and it is especially offensive when untruths are told against someone—it is a sin and it can seriously harm someone's reputation. The *Catechism* states: "This moral prescription flows from the vocation of the holy people to bear witness to their God who is the truth and wills the truth. Offenses against the truth express by word or deed a refusal to commit oneself to moral uprightness: they are fundamental infidelities to God and, in this sense, they undermine the foundations of the covenant" (CCC 2464).

Baptized Christians are called to witness to the truth in word and deed. "The duty of Christians to take part in the life of the Church impels them to act as *witnesses of the Gospel* and of the obligations that flow from it. This witness is a transmission of the faith in words and deeds. Witness is an act of justice that establishes the truth or makes it known" (CCC 2472).

In some rare cases, this witnessing is done in martyrdom. "*Martyrdom* is the supreme witness given to the truth of the faith: it means bearing witness even unto death. The martyr bears witness to Christ who died and rose, to whom he is united by charity. He bears witness to the truth of the faith and of Christian doctrine" (CCC 2473).

REFLECTION QUESTIONS

Ask the children to share their thoughts.

Why should you never say or imply false things about someone?

What are some forms of lies?

What are some things you can avoid so as not to fall into the trap of bearing false witness? List three.

Why is it important never to spread rumors?

CLOSING PRAYER
(to pray together out loud)

Grace After Meals. All of the angels and saints, please pray for us. *Our Father.*

—◆—

Look over the optional activities below and discuss with the family to see if you can carry them out during the upcoming week.

WEEKDAY PRAYER
Each day of the upcoming week at the dinner table, pray this simple prayer.

Dear Lord, Jesus, open my heart to Your love. Blessed Mother, Mary, guide me closer to your Son, Jesus. Amen.

THEME EXTENSION
This activity is for anyone in the family.

Pray for anyone you think has ever said something false about you. Think about any times you might have said something false about someone, and ask God for forgiveness.

EXTRA CREDIT!
This activity is for the entire family.

Sometime this week, take a few moments to plan a simple get-together with relatives, possibly a potluck Sunday luncheon. If you are unable to do so, take the time to talk about your deceased relatives at the dinner table to keep your family memories and traditions alive.

THIRTY-SIX
About the Ninth Commandment

CONTEMPLATE

You shall not covet your neighbor's wife.

—Ninth Commandment

PREPARATIONS

Decide in advance if you'll enlist helpers to assist with making dinner and for help with setting the table. If time allows, read the Contemplate passage and think about it during the day. Also, read the Dinner Table Teaching in advance of your dinner time.

OPENING PRAYER

(to be read out loud by parent or guardian or by all)

Dear Lord, Jesus, please visit our family, blessed with one another and with food to eat. Please take care of those who are lacking in food and do not have a family. *Grace Before Meals. Hail Mary.*

DINNER TABLE TEACHING

Read the Contemplate passage and this Dinner Table Teaching out loud to the family.

This commandment talks to us about the need to remain chaste in thought and deed. Jesus tells us, "Every one who looks at a woman lustfully has already committed adultery with her in his heart" (Matt. 5:28).

We must keep our thoughts pure and avoid the ungodly bombardment coming from the culture. If we become ensnared in indecent movies, television shows, magazines, media, and the like, we are venturing into sinful territory that can lead to sinful thoughts and impure behavior.

The *Catechism* teaches that modesty "guides how one looks at others and behaves toward them in conformity with the dignity of persons and their solidarity" (CCC 2521). Further, "There is a modesty of the feelings as well as of the body. It protests, for example, against the voyeuristic explorations of the human body in certain advertisements, or against the solicitations of certain media that go too far in the exhibition of intimate things. Modesty inspires a way of life which makes it possible to resist the allurements of fashion and the pressures of prevailing ideologies" (CCC 2523).

This gives us very much to ponder. Mother Teresa said, "Purity is the fruit of prayer." We can and should pray that we can practice a modest way of life at all times.

REFLECTION QUESTIONS
Ask the children to share their thoughts.

Why is it important to pray for the grace to be modest and pure?

Will living modestly help to resist allurements and pressures of prevailing ideologies?

Why should you stay clear of impure fashion and media?

CLOSING PRAYER
(to pray together out loud)

Grace After Meals. St. Joseph, patron saint of chastity, please pray for us. *Our Father.*

Look over the optional activities below and discuss with the family to see if you can carry them out during the upcoming week.

WEEKDAY PRAYER
Each day of the upcoming week at the dinner table, pray this simple prayer.

Dear Lord, Jesus, open my heart to your love. St. Joseph, pray for us. Amen.

Also, pray this prayer:

Prayer to St. Joseph
Father and protector of chastity,
glorious St. Joseph,
in whose faithful custody was entrusted the very Innocence,
Jesus Christ and the Virgin of virgins, Mary;
for this twofold and most loved token,
Jesus and Mary,
I pray and plead you to help me always
to purely serve Jesus and Mary
with an uncontaminated soul,
pure heart, and a chaste body.
Amen.

THEME EXTENSION

This activity is for anyone in the family, or it can be carried out together.

During the upcoming week, think about your wardrobe. Are your clothes modest? Can you make some changes even in small increments? Some suggestions are to add a pretty scarf or camisole beneath a neckline that is a bit too low, layer a skirt so the hemline is longer, choose to buy clothing that is not too tight or revealing, and more. You can discuss ideas together.

EXTRA CREDIT!

This activity is for parents or guardians.

Sometime this week, take a few moments to look up a recipe you have never made before that has to do with your heritage. Plan to make it sometime soon for your family's dinner.

THIRTY-SEVEN
About the Tenth Commandment

CONTEMPLATE

You shall not covet your neighbor's goods.
—Tenth Commandment

PREPARATIONS

Decide in advance if you'll enlist helpers to assist with making dinner and for help with setting the table. If time allows, read the Contemplate passage and think about it during the day. Also, read the Dinner Table Teaching in advance of your dinner time.

OPENING PRAYER
(to be read out loud by parent or guardian or by all)

Dear Lord, Jesus, please visit our family, blessed with one another and with food to eat. Please take care of those who are lacking in food and do not have a family. *Grace Before Meals. Hail Mary.*

DINNER TABLE TEACHING

Read the Contemplate passage and this Dinner
Table Teaching out loud to the family.

The tenth commandment forbids greed. "When the Law says, 'You shall not covet,' these words mean that we should banish our desires for whatever does not belong to us. Our thirst for another's goods is immense, infinite, never quenched. Thus it is written: 'He who loves money never has money enough'" (CCC 2536).

We should never be envious of the belongings or achievements of another. We should instead be joyful for others' accomplishments. The Church teaches that envy stems from pride and that we should pray to remain humble. This tenth commandment also forbids greed or amassing earthly goods without limit.

The *Catechism* teaches: "Envy is a capital sin. It refers to the sadness at the sight of another's goods and the immoderate desire to acquire them for oneself, even unjustly. When it wishes grave harm to a neighbor it is a mortal sin" (CCC 2539). St. Gregory the Great said, "From envy are born hatred, detraction, calumny, joy caused by the misfortune of a neighbor, and displeasure caused by his prosperity" (CCC 2539).

Our protection against envy, the Church instructs, comes "through good-will, humility, and abandonment to the providence of God" (CCC 2554).

REFLECTION QUESTIONS

Ask the children to share their thoughts.

List three ways that you might covet your neighbor's goods.

Why should you not covet anyone or their belongings?

What are some ways that you can prevent this from happening?

CLOSING PRAYER
(to pray together out loud)

Grace After Meals. All of the angels and saints, please pray for us. *Our Father.*

———————

Look over the optional activities below and discuss with the family to see if you can carry them out during the upcoming week.

WEEKDAY PRAYER
Each day of the upcoming week at the dinner table, pray this simple prayer.

Dear Lord, Jesus, open my heart to Your love. Help me to be more giving and never fall into the trap of the devil to covet anything from anyone. Amen.

THEME EXTENSION
This activity is for anyone in the family.

During the upcoming week, notice if you might be coveting anything or anyone. Take it to prayer—ask God to forgive you if you have sinned, and pray for humility and the willingness to abandon yourself to the providence of God.

EXTRA CREDIT!
This activity is for the entire family.

Sometime this week, go to the sacrament of Confession.

• R E C I P E •

Meatloaf

My friend Fran Speede shares her meatloaf recipe. This recipe may seem very simple, but it is delicious. The best thing about its simplicity is that you can put it together fairly quickly. Fran tells me: "My best friend Denise gave this recipe to me years ago. I tweak it a little bit every time I make it, and I think of her."

Ingredients
- 1½ lbs. ground beef or ground turkey
- 2 eggs
- 1 8-oz. can of tomato sauce
- ¾ cup of bread crumbs
- 1 packet of dry onion soup mix

Directions
Mix all ingredients together in a large bowl. Place in a baking dish. Bake at 350°F for 1 hour. Enjoy!

THIRTY-EIGHT
Learning the Love of Family from Sts. Zélie and Louis Martin

CONTEMPLATE

The holy spouses Louis Martin and Marie-Azélie Guérin practiced Christian service in the family, creating day by day an environment of faith and love which nurtured the vocations of their daughters, among whom was St. Thérèse of the Child Jesus.

—Pope Francis[28]

PREPARATIONS

Decide in advance if you'll enlist helpers to assist with making dinner and for help with setting the table. If time allows, read the Contemplate passage and think about it during the day. Also, read the Dinner Table Teaching in advance of your dinner time.

OPENING PRAYER

(to be read out loud by parent or guardian or by all)

Dear Lord, Jesus, please visit our family, blessed with one another and with food to eat. Please take care of those who are lacking in food and do not have a family. *Grace Before Meals. Hail Mary.*

DINNER TABLE TEACHING

Read the Contemplate passage and this Dinner
Table Teaching out loud to the family.

Sts. Zélie and Louis Martin are the first-ever married couple with children to be canonized in the same ceremony. Pope Francis presided over the Mass with their Rite of Canonization at St. Peter's Square on October 18, 2015.

Louis Joseph Aloys Stanislaus Martin and Marie-Azélie Guérin were both born in France. Before meeting one another, they each possessed similar aspirations. Both Louis, a watchmaker by trade, and Zélie, a very talented lace maker, set out to enter religious vocations. But both were unsuccessful. Louis had trouble learning Latin, and Zélie was turned away from the convent due to health reasons. God was calling them to the married vocation. They met in Alençon, France, got to know one another and became engaged, and were married in 1858 when Louis was thirty-four and Zélie was twenty-six. Over the next fifteen years, Zélie gave birth to seven girls and two boys.

"We lived only for them; they were all our happiness," Zélie wrote.[29] But sadly the couple lost their two baby boys, a five-year-old daughter, and a baby girl. Their steadfast faith sustained them, though they were filled with sorrow.

When her sister-in-law lost an infant son, Zélie reached out to comfort her. She wrote: "When I closed the eyes of my dear little children and buried them, I felt sorrow through and through. . . . People said to me, 'It would have been better never to have had them.' I couldn't stand such language. My children were not lost forever; life is short and full of miseries, and we shall find our little ones again up above."[30]

Louis and Zélie raised their children with much love and training in the Christian faith. All five daughters joined the religious life and were professed nuns. St. Thérèse of Lisieux, Doctor of the Church, is one of them.

REFLECTION QUESTIONS

Ask the children to share their thoughts.

Do hardships and losses necessarily mean that everything will fail? Think about the fact that both Louis and Zélie were turned away from religious life, and that they lost four children.

How might acceptance of God's will help one in life?

How did Louis and Zélie succeed at raising their five daughters in the faith?

CLOSING PRAYER

(to pray together out loud)

Grace After Meals. Sts. Louis and Zélie Martin, please pray for us. *Our Father.*

Look over the optional activities below and discuss with the family to see if you can carry them out during the upcoming week.

WEEKDAY PRAYER

Each day of the upcoming week at the dinner table, pray this simple prayer.

Dear Lord, Jesus, open my heart to Your love. Sts. Louis and Zélie, teach me love of family. Amen.

THEME EXTENSION

This activity is for anyone in the family.

Whenever you experience any negativity, doubt, or challenge regarding family life, call upon Sts. Louis and Zélie Martin in prayer.

EXTRA CREDIT!
This activity is for anyone in the family.

Sometime this week, take a few moments to research the lives of the Martin family. You can start here: www.littleflower.org/therese/life-story/. Then, when time allows, share what you have learned with your family at the dinner table.

• RECIPE •

Potato Cakes (Side Dish)

This fun recipe is not only delicious but makes good use of leftover mashed potatoes. My daughter Jessica told me about her basic recipe, and I have changed it up many times since first trying it out.

Ingredients

- leftover mashed potatoes, whatever amount you have (hopefully at least 2 cups)
- 1 clove fresh garlic, minced
- 1 medium red onion, finely chopped
- 1–2 cups bread crumbs (as needed to arrive at the right consistency for forming into patties)
- 1 egg
- 1 whole scallion with green, chopped (optional)
- salt and pepper to taste
- olive oil for frying
- 2 or 3 slices of cooked turkey bacon, chopped (optional)

Directions

Sauté the garlic and onions in a little olive oil. If you are using turkey bacon and it is not yet cooked, cook it with the garlic and onion. If it is already cooked, add it at the end just to warm. When everything is cooked, remove from pan.

Add sautéed garlic, onion, and bacon to the mashed potatoes and egg in a large glass or stainless steel mixing bowl. Add the minced scallion if you are including it. Mix well, slowly adding bread crumbs until it is a good consistency for making into thin patties. Add salt and pepper to taste.

Warm some olive oil (or other oil) in a cast iron or other sturdy pan. You can reuse the pan from sautéing the garlic and onion. Form potato cakes in your hands from the mixture. Place two or three potato cakes in the pan at a time, and watch carefully to turn when they are golden brown. After turning, watch closely again until the other side is cooked and light brown, and then place on a plate lined with a paper towel. You may place them in a low-temperature oven to keep warm while making the rest.

These potato cakes make a nice side dish for any meal. They also go well with an egg breakfast. Enjoy!

THIRTY-NINE
Learning about Prayer from the Saints

CONTEMPLATE

For me, prayer is a surge of the heart; it is a simple look turned toward heaven, it is a cry of recognition and of love, embracing both trial and joy.

—St. Thérèse of Lisieux, *The Story of a Soul*

PREPARATIONS

Decide in advance if you'll enlist helpers to assist with making dinner and for help with setting the table. If time allows, read the Contemplate passage and think about it during the day. Also, read the Dinner Table Teaching in advance of your dinner time.

OPENING PRAYER
(to be read out loud by parent or guardian or by all)

Dear Lord, Jesus, please visit our family, blessed with one another and with food to eat. Please take care of those who are lacking in food and do not have a family. *Grace Before Meals. Hail Mary.*

DINNER TABLE TEACHING

Read the Contemplate passage and this Dinner
Table Teaching out loud to the family.

Essentially every religion has at its core humanity's innate search for God. God created men and women and has tirelessly called each person to Himself. St. Teresa of Calcutta often expressed that God *thirsts* for our love. The Church teaches: "Whether we know it or not, prayer is the encounter of God's thirst with ours. God thirsts that we may thirst for him" (CCC 2560).

St. Thérèse tells us, "Prayer is a surge of the heart." We reach our hearts up to God through trial and joy. Similarly, St. John Damascene says, "Prayer is the raising of one's mind and heart to God or the requesting of good things from God" (CCC 2559).

St. Augustine wrote that "man is a beggar before God" (CCC 2559). We must admit that we can't pray as we should (see Rom. 8:26). It is from a contrite and humble heart that we can receive the gift of prayer from God.

We are in communion with God through our Baptism. The *Catechism* teaches that the life of prayer is the habit of being in the presence of God (see CCC 2565). We can form habits of prayer by making the time for it in our busy lives. At certain times throughout the day, we raise our hearts to God. And sometimes we feel an urgent need to seek his help.

St. Teresa of Ávila reminds us, "Prayer is nothing else than being on terms of friendship with God."[31] Let's be sure to make the time for prayer and stay in friendship with God.

REFLECTION QUESTIONS

Ask the children to share their thoughts.

Why should we pray?

When should we pray? Only when we need something from God?

Can anyone pray?

How should we be when we pray?

CLOSING PRAYER
(to pray together out loud)

Grace After Meals. All of the angels and saints, please pray for us. *Our Father.*

———

Look over the optional activities below and discuss with the family to see if you can carry them out during the upcoming week.

WEEKDAY PRAYER
Each day of the upcoming week at the dinner table, pray this simple prayer.

Dear Lord, Jesus, open my heart to Your love. St. Thérèse, St. Augustine, St. John Damascene, St. Teresa, and all of the saints, please teach us how to pray. Amen.

THEME EXTENSION
This activity is for anyone in the family.

Make a point to pause and pray often. This can be done even when busy with work or play—pause interiorly and raise your heart to God.

EXTRA CREDIT!
This activity is for anyone in the family.

Sometime this week, take a few moments to research a favorite or lesser-known saint and learn about his or her prayer life. Share what you have learned with your family at the dinner table.

FORTY

Learning to Pray from Jesus

CONTEMPLATE

When Jesus prays he is already teaching us how to pray. His prayer to his Father is the theological path (the path of faith, hope, and charity) of our prayer to God.

—CCC 2607

PREPARATIONS

Decide in advance if you'll enlist helpers to assist with making dinner and for help with setting the table. If time allows, read the Contemplate passage and think about it during the day. Also, read the Dinner Table Teaching in advance of your dinner time.

OPENING PRAYER

(to be read out loud by parent or guardian or by all)

Dear Lord, Jesus, please visit our family, blessed with one another and with food to eat. Please take care of those who are lacking in food and do not have a family. *Grace Before Meals. Hail Mary.*

DINNER TABLE TEACHING

Read the Contemplate passage and this Dinner
Table Teaching out loud to the family.

No doubt the Blessed Mother taught Jesus about prayer when He was a little boy. He would also have learned about prayer in the synagogue in Nazareth and the temple in Jerusalem. At the young age of twelve, He said, "I must be in my Father's house" (Lk. 2:49).

The Gospels speak about Jesus always praying prior to major moments in His own ministry and the mission of His apostles. He also went away in solitude to pray to His Father.

Jesus meets us where we are at in our lives, and leads us to his Father. The followers of Jesus learned to pray by watching their Master. They were eager to learn and asked Him, "Lord, teach us to pray" (Lk. 11:1). Jesus insists that we always reconcile with our brothers and neighbors before approaching God. He calls us all to a conversion of heart and asks us to pray with a lively and persevering faith: "Whatever you ask in prayer, believe that you receive it, and you will" (Mk. 11:24).

Jesus teaches us prayer through His example. We see that He was obedient to His Father's will, praying always with wholehearted faith and confidence. The *Catechism* teaches, "Jesus' filial prayer is the perfect model of prayer in the New Testament. Often done in solitude and in secret, the prayer of Jesus involves a loving adherence to the will of the Father even to the Cross and an absolute confidence in being heard" (CCC 2620).

REFLECTION QUESTIONS

Ask the children to share their thoughts.

List some ways that Jesus teaches us to pray.

Why should we reconcile with others before praying? Can we pray for grace and strength to reconcile with others?

Why should we pray with faith?

Share ways that you pray.

CLOSING PRAYER

(to pray together out loud)

Grace After Meals. Blessed Mother, Mary, please pray for us. *Our Father.*

———

Look over the optional activities below and discuss with the family to see if you can carry them out during the upcoming week.

WEEKDAY PRAYER

Each day of the upcoming week at the dinner table, pray this simple prayer.

Dear Lord, Jesus, open my heart to Your love. Teach me to pray with a sincere heart and a lively faith. Amen.

THEME EXTENSION

This activity is for anyone in the family.

If possible, find some times to move away from the noisiness of the day and retreat to quiet prayer.

EXTRA CREDIT!

This activity is for the entire family.

Sometime this week, spend some time with Jesus in the Blessed Sacrament at church or in an Adoration chapel.

———

FORTY-ONE
Learning to Pray from the Blessed Mother

CONTEMPLATE

The Gospel reveals to us how Mary prays and intercedes in faith. At Cana, the mother of Jesus asks her son for the needs of a wedding feast; this is the sign of another feast—that of the wedding of the Lamb where he gives his body and blood at the request of the Church, his Bride. It is at the hour of the New Covenant, at the foot of the cross, that Mary is heard as the Woman, the new Eve, the true "Mother of all the living."

—CCC 2618

PREPARATIONS

Decide in advance if you'll enlist helpers to assist with making dinner and for help with setting the table. If time allows, read the Contemplate passage and think about it during the day. Also, read the Dinner Table Teaching in advance of your dinner time.

OPENING PRAYER

(to be read out loud by parent or guardian or by all)

Dear Lord, Jesus, please visit our family, blessed with one another and with food to eat. Please take care of those who are lacking in food and do not have a family. *Grace Before Meals. Hail Mary.*

DINNER TABLE TEACHING

Read the Contemplate passage and this Dinner Table Teaching out loud to the family.

The Blessed Mother fully consented in faith to be the Mother of God when she gave her "yes" or *fiat* to the angel Gabriel who appeared to her at the Annunciation: "Behold, I am the handmaid of the Lord; let it be [done] to me according to your word" (Lk. 1:38). She was steadfast in her faithful consent all the way to the cross of her Son, Jesus. She remains steadfast still as our Mother from heaven. When Jesus hung from the cross, He entrusted His Mother, Mary, to the whole world: "Behold, your mother!"(John 19:27).

The Church teaches: "Because of Mary's singular cooperation with the action of the Holy Spirit, the Church loves to pray in communion with the Virgin Mary, to magnify with her the great things the Lord has done for her, and to entrust supplications and praises to her" (CCC 2682).

Mary's example teaches us to be resolute in our prayers. Even though she was destined to be the Mother of God, she was first a faithful young Jewish girl who chose to pray and follow the teachings of her faith. When a couple was without wine for their wedding feast, Mary asked her Son, Jesus, to take care of them and then told the wine stewards, "Do whatever he tells you" (John 2:5). Her message is the same to us. We need to follow her Son, Jesus, and do what He tells us. Prayers to Mary bring us closer to her Son because, in Mary's humility, she always points toward her Son.

REFLECTION QUESTIONS

Ask the children to share their thoughts.

What kinds of virtues do you think the Blessed Mother exemplified?

How can we emulate the Blessed Mother in her faith and prayer?

Should we ever hesitate to pray to Mary?

What do you think Mary can do for you? How can she help you?

CLOSING PRAYER

(to pray together out loud)

Grace After Meals. Blessed Mother, Mary, please pray for us. *Our Father.*

———

Look over the optional activities below and discuss with the family to see if you can carry them out during the upcoming week.

WEEKDAY PRAYER

Each day of the upcoming week at the dinner table, pray this simple prayer.

Dear Lord, Jesus, open my heart to Your love. Blessed Mother, Mary, teach me to be steadfast and loving in my prayers. Amen.

Add the Memorare prayer if you would like:

Memorare

Remember, O most gracious Virgin Mary, that never was it known that anyone who fled to thy protection, implored thy help, or sought thine intercession was left unaided.

Inspired by this confidence, I fly unto thee, O Virgin of virgins, my mother; to thee do I come, before thee I stand, sinful and sorrowful. O Mother of the Word Incarnate, despise not my petitions, but in thy mercy hear and answer me. Amen.

THEME EXTENSION

This activity is for anyone in the family, or it can be carried out together.

Pray the Hail Mary very slowly. Think of each word or each group of words.

EXTRA CREDIT!

This activity is for anyone in the family.

Sometime this week, take a few moments to do some spiritual reading about the Blessed Mother from a Church-approved source.

FORTY-TWO
Learning to Pray from the Holy Spirit

CONTEMPLATE

The Church invites us to call upon the Holy Spirit every day, especially at the beginning and end of every important action.
—CCC 2670

PREPARATIONS

Decide in advance if you'll enlist helpers to assist with making dinner and for help with setting the table. If time allows, read the Contemplate passage and think about it during the day. Also, read the Dinner Table Teaching in advance of your dinner time.

OPENING PRAYER
(to be read out loud by parent or guardian or by all)

Dear Lord, Jesus, please visit our family, blessed with one another and with food to eat. Please take care of those who are lacking in food and do not have a family. *Grace Before Meals. Hail Mary.*

DINNER TABLE TEACHING

Read the Contemplate passage and this Dinner
Table Teaching out loud to the family.

We are familiar with the prayer, "Come, Holy Spirit, fill the hearts of your faithful and kindle in them the fire of your love" (*Roman Missal,* Pentecost Alleluia verse). The Holy Spirit or Third Person of the Holy Trinity is commonly invoked. Praying to the Holy Spirit has been developed in antiphons and hymns in every liturgical tradition.

Jesus promised the arrival of the Holy Spirit who was sent by the Father and who will remain with us. At Pentecost the Holy Spirit came to the Blessed Mother and the twelve apostles who had been waiting and praying in the upper room after Jesus was crucified. The Holy Spirit continually guides the Church and guides us all.

The Holy Spirit is also the interior Master of Christian prayer. The *Catechism* says: "To be sure, there are as many paths of prayer as there are persons who pray, but it is the same Spirit acting in all and with all" (CCC 2674). So, "the Church invites us to invoke the Holy Spirit as the interior Teacher of Christian prayer" (CCC 2681). We should not hesitate to ask the Holy Spirit to teach us to pray and to help us when we might be at a loss for words. In fact, the Holy Spirit even prays for us, as we learn in St. Paul's Letter to the Romans: "The Spirit helps us in our weakness; for we do not know how to pray as we ought, but the Spirit himself intercedes for us with sighs too deep for words" (Rom. 8:26).

REFLECTION QUESTIONS

Ask the children to share their thoughts.

Who is the Holy Spirit?

How does the Holy Spirit teach you to pray?

Who guides the Church?

Why should you seek help from the Holy Spirit?

CLOSING PRAYER

(to pray together out loud)

Grace After Meals. Holy Spirit, please enlighten us. *Our Father.*

———

Look over the optional activities below and discuss with the family to see if you can carry them out during the upcoming week.

WEEKDAY PRAYER

Each day of the upcoming week at the dinner table, pray this simple prayer.

Dear Lord, Jesus, open my heart to Your love. Holy Spirit, please teach me to pray as I ought. Amen.

THEME EXTENSION

This activity is for anyone in the family, or it can be carried out together.

During the upcoming week, pray this prayer to the Holy Spirit and take a few moments to pause and reflect:

St. Augustine's Prayer to the Holy Spirit

Breathe in me, O Holy Spirit, that my thoughts may all be holy. Act in me, O Holy Spirit, that my work, too, may be holy. Draw my heart, O Holy Spirit, that I love but what is holy. Strengthen me, O Holy Spirit, to defend all that is holy. Guard me, then, O Holy Spirit, that I always may be holy. Amen.

This activity is for anyone in the family.

Sometime this week, take a few moments to read the Catechism paragraphs 694–701 to learn about the symbols of the Holy Spirit: water, anointing, fire, cloud and light, the seal, the hand, the finger, and the dove.

• RECIPE •

Homemade Tomato Soup

My friend Barb Scholten shares her recipe for a delicious classic tomato soup. She says it is easily doubled or tripled, and it freezes well. Barb says: "It is wonderful for children to know how tomato soup is made. It doesn't always come from a can!"

Ingredients

- 1 medium onion, chopped
- 2 tbsp. olive oil
- 2 tsp. minced garlic
- 1 can diced tomatoes
- 1 tsp. dried oregano
- 1 tsp. dried basil
- 1 tsp. apple cider vinegar
- 1 cup vegetable broth
- ½ cup milk or light cream (almond milk can be substituted for those avoiding dairy)
- shredded cheese or croutons, to garnish top of soup when served (optional)

Directions

Heat a large greased or nonstick pot over medium-high heat. Add a couple of tablespoons of extra virgin olive oil (or whatever oil you prefer.) When oil is hot, add onion and cook, stirring occasionally, until golden, about 5 minutes. Stir in the minced garlic and cook for another minute. Add the tomatoes, oregano, basil, and apple cider vinegar, and bring to boil. Once the mixture is boiling, add the broth and milk or cream and bring to a boil once again.

Using an immersion blender, puree the soup until smooth. (If you don't have an immersion blender, puree the soup in batches in a standing blender.) Salt and pepper to taste. Pour the soup into four bowls, top with your shredded cheese or croutons if desired, and serve. Enjoy!

FORTY-THREE
Kinds of Prayer

CONTEMPLATE

Whether or not our prayer is heard depends not on the number
of words, but on the fervor of our souls.
— St. John Chrysostom (CCC 2700)

PREPARATIONS

*Decide in advance if you'll enlist helpers to assist with making dinner and
for help with setting the table. If time allows, read the Contemplate passage and
think about it during the day. Also, read the Dinner Table Teaching in advance
of your dinner time.*

OPENING PRAYER
(to be read out loud by parent or guardian or by all)

Dear Lord, Jesus, please visit our family, blessed with one another and
with food to eat. Please take care of those who are lacking in food and do
not have a family. *Grace Before Meals. Hail Mary.*

DINNER TABLE TEACHING
*Read the Contemplate passage and this Dinner
Table Teaching out loud to the family.*

Sometimes our prayer is more formal; many times it is simple and heartfelt. Whatever our prayer, it should always be voiced from a sincere and humble heart. God will never fail to hear our earnest and loving prayers.

The Church teaches: "Through his Word, God speaks to man. By words, mental or vocal, our prayer takes flesh. Yet it is most important that the heart should be present to him to whom we are speaking in prayer" (CCC 2700). As St. John Chrysostom said, "Whether or not our prayer is heard depends not on the number of words, but on the fervor of our souls."

The Church tells us that there are three expressions for prayer: vocal, meditative, and contemplative. "Vocal prayer is an essential element of the Christian life" (CCC 2701). Jesus illustrated vocal prayer when He taught his disciples to pray the Our Father. We vocalize to express the prayers that rise up from our hearts for love of God.

The *Catechism* calls meditative prayer a "quest" that engages our thought, imagination, emotion, and desire. "The mind seeks to understand the why and how of the Christian life, in order to adhere and respond to what the Lord is asking" (CCC 2705). Aids for meditative prayers include books, Scripture, liturgical texts of the day or season, holy images, icons, and more. These images and words can help us to be less distracted and more focused in our prayers.

In contemplative prayer, we spend time with the Lord. "Contemplative prayer is the simple expression of the mystery of prayer. It is a gaze of faith fixed on Jesus, an attentiveness to the Word of God, a silent love. It achieves real union with the prayer of Christ to the extent that it makes us share in his mystery" (CCC 2724).

We humble ourselves before him, pour out our hearts to him, and take the time to listen to him speak to our souls. St. Teresa of Ávila explained simply: "Contemplative prayer in my opinion is nothing else than a close sharing between friends; it means taking time frequently to be alone with him who we know loves us" (CCC 2709).

REFLECTION QUESTIONS

Ask the children to share their thoughts.

What are some kinds of prayer?

What is most important when we pray?

What kinds of things can help us to meditate when we pray?

When should you pray?

CLOSING PRAYER

(to pray together out loud)

Grace After Meals. St. Teresa of Ávila, please pray for us. *Our Father.*

———

Look over the optional activities below and discuss with the family to see if you can carry them out during the upcoming week.

WEEKDAY PRAYER

Each day of the upcoming week at the dinner table, pray this simple prayer.

Dear Lord, Jesus, open my heart to Your love. St. Teresa of Ávila, teach me to pray. Amen.

THEME EXTENSION

This activity is for anyone in the family.

When there is a break in your schedule, strive to pause and recollect yourself to pray silently yet fervently to the Lord. When there is no break in your schedule, take a moment anyway to pause—even briefly—and offer your heart to God.

EXTRA CREDIT!

This activity is for anyone in the family.

Sometime this week, take a few moments to find a sacred object and carve out a little quiet time to pray and meditate. For instance, if you choose a crucifix, you can pray and meditate about Christ's Passion and death on the cross. If you choose words in Sacred Scripture, slowly read one or two lines a few times, and ask God to show you what they mean. You might gaze upon a sacred icon—pictured in an art book or hanging in your home or at church—and thank God for his great love for you. If you choose a statue of the Blessed Mother, gaze upon it while praying for her help in your life, asking her to bring you closer to her Son, Jesus.

Whatever way you pray, be sure to pause and allow quiet time for our Lord to speak to your heart.

FORTY-FOUR
Favorable Places to Pray

CONTEMPLATE

The most appropriate places for prayer are personal or family oratories, monasteries, places of pilgrimage, and above all the church, which is the proper place for liturgical prayer for the parish community and the privileged place for Eucharistic adoration.

—CCC 2696

PREPARATIONS

Decide in advance if you'll enlist helpers to assist with making dinner and for help with setting the table. If time allows, read the Contemplate passage and think about it during the day. Also, read the Dinner Table Teaching in advance of your dinner time.

OPENING PRAYER
(to be read out loud by parent or guardian or by all)

Dear Lord, Jesus, please visit our family, blessed with one another and with food to eat. Please take care of those who are lacking in food and do not have a family. *Grace Before Meals. Hail Mary.*

DINNER TABLE TEACHING

Read the Contemplate passage and this Dinner
Table Teaching out loud to the family.

We can pray no matter where we are. We can always offer prayers; even if there are rules in place that prohibit prayer, we can still pray silently. No one can force another to keep from praying, and God is always listening.

Still, the Church recommends favorable places to pray. The *Catechism* mentions monasteries, pilgrimage sites, and churches (see CCC 2696), but it also says:

"The *Christian family* is the first place of education in prayer. Based on the sacrament of marriage, the family is the 'domestic church' where God's children learn to pray 'as the Church' and to persevere in prayer. For young children in particular, daily family prayer is the first witness of the Church's living memory as awakened patiently by the Holy Spirit" (CCC 2685).

Parents can create a prayer corner or prayer table in their domestic church where sacred images and sacramentals such as rosary beads are placed and where prayer becomes more tangible. A prayer "oratory" such as this can help foster communal prayer. And families can pray together when gathered at the dinner table, as you are doing when using this book. Family prayer can occur when traveling—any time you are gathered together.

Of course, we also pray individually and as a family in church when we attend Mass and other liturgical services. We pray with the Church, the Body of Christ, when we pray in union with others—praying the prayers of the Church throughout the world. We also might pray the Liturgy of the Hours at different times of the day.

A pilgrimage can be a special occasion for a renewal of prayer and a conversion of heart. It helps us focus on heaven and its rewards. We can take part in a prayerful pilgrimage to a shrine or a holy place with other Christians or with our families.

REFLECTION QUESTIONS
Ask the children to share their thoughts.

List some favorable places to pray.

Is it necessary to be in a certain place to pray?

Is there a place or places where you cannot pray?

CLOSING PRAYER
(to pray together out loud)

Grace After Meals. Blessed Mother, Mary, please pray for us. *Our Father.*

Look over the optional activities below and discuss with the family to see if you can carry them out during the upcoming week.

WEEKDAY PRAYER
Each day of the upcoming week at the dinner table, pray this simple prayer.

Dear Lord, Jesus, open my heart to Your love. Blessed Mother, Mary, and all of the saints and angels, please guide us in prayer. Amen.

THEME EXTENSION
This activity is for anyone in the family.

Find extra opportunities to pray.

EXTRA CREDIT!

This activity is for the entire family.

Sometime this week, take a few moments to plan a potluck Rosary night. Invite relatives or friends from your parish. Ask each person to bring a covered side dish to share. Pray the Rosary together either before or after dinner. You will be creating wonderful memories for your family.

• RECIPE •

Russian Teacakes

This recipe makes four dozen cookies.

My sister-in-law Karen Cooper shares her traditional Russian teacake recipe. For about forty years, Karen has baked a huge platter of these cookies each Christmas. I have been a happy recipient for a number of Christmases. She started when she was only fifteen, alongside her mother. Karen reminisces: "It was so special because we spent time together and it was just me and my Mom."

My children and I love to bake Russian teacakes as well, and because they are so delicious, they are one of our favorite kinds of holiday cookies.

Ingredients
- 1 cup soft butter
- ½ cup sifted confectioner's sugar
- 1 tsp. vanilla
- 2¼ cups sifted flour
- ¼ tsp. salt
- ¾ cup walnuts, finely chopped

Directions

Mix butter, sugar, and vanilla thoroughly. Separately, sift together flour and
salt and stir, and then mix in walnuts. Combine wet and dry ingredients.
Chill dough.

Roll dough into 1-inch balls. Place on an ungreased baking sheet. (Cookies
will not spread.) Bake at 400°F until set, but not brown, for about 10–12
min.

While they are still warm, roll the cookies in confectioner's sugar. Let cool.
Roll in sugar again. Enjoy!

FORTY-FIVE
The Desire for God

CONTEMPLATE

The desire for God is written in the human heart, because man is created by God and for God; and God never ceases to draw man to himself. Only in God will he find the truth and happiness he never stops searching for.

—CCC 27

PREPARATIONS

Decide in advance if you'll enlist helpers to assist with making dinner and for help with setting the table. If time allows, read the Contemplate passage and think about it during the day. Also, read the Dinner Table Teaching in advance of your dinner time.

OPENING PRAYER
(to be read out loud by parent or guardian or by all)

Dear Lord, Jesus, please visit our family, blessed with one another and with food to eat. Please take care of those who are lacking in food and do not have a family. *Grace Before Meals. Hail Mary.*

DINNER TABLE TEACHING

Read the Contemplate passage and this Dinner
Table Teaching out loud to the family.

St. Augustine is known for having said, "You have made us for yourself, O Lord, and our hearts are restless until they rest in you."[32] As you have learned in another lesson, St. Augustine was a brilliant man who spent much of his early life away from God. His mother, St. Monica, prayed intensely for his coming to the faith. He realized that the pleasures of the world were not enough—they did not give rest to his soul. He was converted and became a powerful witness to the gospel. He was eventually canonized a saint and proclaimed a Doctor of the Church.

We all have a deep yearning and desire to be in union with our loving God, to get to know Him more intimately and to rest in His love. Throughout history and down to our present day, humanity has been on a quest for God, as is seen through religious practices and beliefs. But, humanity has also rejected God and fallen away from Him. This can happen by getting caught up with the messages of the sinful culture of the world, by associating with and becoming influenced by nonbelievers, and by not nourishing our faith with sound Church teaching and with regular reception of the sacraments.

Take time to get to know God more intimately through study, continual prayer, and frequent participation in the sacraments of the Church.

REFLECTION QUESTIONS

Ask the children to share their thoughts.

Why do we long for God?

What steps can you take to remain in God's friendship?

Is there something you can do to help inspire others to yearn for God? Take time to discuss.

CLOSING PRAYER
(to pray together out loud)

Grace After Meals. Dear Holy Trinity, Father, Son, and Holy Spirit, please pray for us. *Our Father.*

———

Look over the optional activities below and discuss with the family to see if you can carry them out during the upcoming week.

WEEKDAY PRAYER
Each day of the upcoming week at the dinner table, pray this simple prayer.

Dear Lord, Jesus, open my heart to Your love. Blessed Mother, Mary, keep me free from evil. Amen.

THEME EXTENSION
This activity is for anyone in the family.

Take time to think of God, and pray to become more aware of His presence in your life.

EXTRA CREDIT!
This activity is for anyone in the family.

Sometime this week, take a few moments to ponder ways your family can be instrumental in helping another family who you think might be struggling with their connection to God.

———

FORTY-SIX
Sacred Scripture

CONTEMPLATE

In Sacred Scripture, the Church constantly finds her nourishment and her strength, for she welcomes it not as a human word, "but as what it really is, the word of God."

—CCC 104

PREPARATIONS

Decide in advance if you'll enlist helpers to assist with making dinner and for help with setting the table. If time allows, read the Contemplate passage and think about it during the day. Also, read the Dinner Table Teaching in advance of your dinner time.

OPENING PRAYER
(to be read out loud by parent or guardian or by all)

Dear Lord, Jesus, please visit our family, blessed with one another and with food to eat. Please take care of those who are lacking in food and do not have a family. *Grace Before Meals. Hail Mary.*

DINNER TABLE TEACHING
Read the Contemplate passage and this Dinner Table Teaching out loud to the family.

Sacred Scripture is authored by God, who has inspired the human authors of the Old and New Testaments. St. Augustine says, "You recall that one and the same Word of God extends throughout Scripture, that it is one and the same Utterance that resounds in the mouths of all the sacred writers, since he who was in the beginning God with God has no need of separate syllables; for he is not subject to time" (CCC 102).

The Second Vatican Council document *Dei Verbum* (God's Word) states: "For holy mother Church, relying on the belief of the Apostles, holds that the books of both the Old and New Testaments in their entirety, with all their parts, are sacred and canonical because written under the inspiration of the Holy Spirit, they have God as their author and have been handed on as such to the Church herself."[33]

Sacred Scripture nourishes our souls; it teaches and guides us. All preaching, catechetics, and Christian instruction should thrive and get its nourishment from Sacred Scripture. As we read in the Psalms, "Your word is a lamp to my feet and a light to my path" (Ps. 119:105 NRSV).

REFLECTION QUESTIONS

Ask the children to share their thoughts.

Why is Sacred Scripture important?

Who is the author of Sacred Scripture?

How can we trust that the words are authentic?

How might you pray with Sacred Scripture?

CLOSING PRAYER

(to pray together out loud)

Grace After Meals. Sts. Matthew, Mark, Luke, and John, please pray for us. *Our Father.*

———●———

Look over the optional activities below and discuss with the family to see if you can carry them out during the upcoming week.

WEEKDAY PRAYER

Each day of the upcoming week at the dinner table, pray this simple prayer.

Dear Lord, Jesus, open my heart to Your love. Blessed Mother, Mary, bring me closer to your Son, Jesus. Amen.

THEME EXTENSION

This activity is for anyone in the family.

During the upcoming week, choose a passage of Sacred Scripture and read it slowly a few times. Pray about it and be quiet, allowing our Lord to speak to your heart about its meaning.

EXTRA CREDIT!

This activity is for the entire family.

Sometime this week, take a few moments to contact a relative and arrange a visit.

———●———

FORTY-SEVEN
Why Catholics Honor the Blessed Mother

CONTEMPLATE

At one point I began to question my devotion to Mary, believing that, if it became too great, it might end up compromising the supremacy of the worship owed to Christ. At that time, I was greatly helped by a book by Saint Louis Marie de Montfort. . . . There I found the answers to my questions. Yes, Mary does bring us closer to Christ; she does lead us to him, provided that we live her mystery in Christ. . . . The author was an outstanding theologian. His Mariological thought is rooted in the mystery of the Trinity and in the truth of the Incarnation of the Word of God.

—Pope John Paul II, *Gift and Mystery*[34]

PREPARATIONS

Decide in advance if you'll enlist helpers to assist with making dinner and for help with setting the table. If time allows, read the Contemplate passage and think about it during the day. Also, read the Dinner Table Teaching in advance of your dinner time.

OPENING PRAYER

(to be read out loud by parent or guardian or by all)

Dear Lord, Jesus, please visit our family, blessed with one another and with food to eat. Please take care of those who are lacking in food and do not have a family. *Grace Before Meals. Hail Mary.*

DINNER TABLE TEACHING

*Read the Contemplate passage and this Dinner
Table Teaching out loud to the family.*

Catholics honor Mary and also ask for her intercession and prayers on their behalf. "Because of Mary's singular cooperation with the action of the Holy Spirit, the Church loves to pray in communion with the Virgin Mary, to magnify with her the great things the Lord has done for her, and to entrust supplications and praises to her" (CCC 2682).

Catholics worship God; they *honor* God's Mother, Mary. We know that the Blessed Mother played an absolutely essential role in salvation history. Her wholehearted generous "yes" enabled the Holy Spirit to work in her to bring about the birth of the Son of God. When Mary's Son, Jesus, hung on the cross, he gave the world the great gift of His Mother when He said, "Here is your mother" (John 19:27 NRSV).

Since Mary is Mother to all humankind, it is only fitting and natural that we honor her with our love and prayers. At the wedding feast in Cana when there was no wine, Mary told the servants, "Do whatever he tells you" (John 2:5), meaning they should listen attentively to her Son, Jesus. Her instruction is the same for us. She is always directing everyone to her Son, Jesus. As St. John Paul II says, "Yes, Mary does bring us closer to Christ; she does lead us to him, provided that we live her mystery in Christ."[35]

REFLECTION QUESTIONS

Ask the children to share their thoughts.

Why should we give honor to the Blessed Mother?

How can Mary help you when you pray to her?

What are some ways in which you can honor Mother Mary? List three.

CLOSING PRAYER

(to pray together out loud)

Grace After Meals. Blessed Mother, Mary, please pray for us. *Our Father.*

Look over the optional activities below and discuss with the family to see if you can carry them out during the upcoming week.

WEEKDAY PRAYER

Each day of the upcoming week at the dinner table, pray this simple prayer.

Dear Lord, Jesus, open my heart to Your love. Blessed Virgin Mary, Mother of God, show me the way to get closer to your Son. Amen.

THEME EXTENSION

This activity is for anyone in the family, or it can be carried out together.

Read Luke 1:26–55. Take some time to reflect on the words. Perhaps someone can read the passages at the dinner table one night in the upcoming week.

Sometime this week, take a few moments to plan a way for your family to honor Mary: maybe planting a flower garden in honor of Mary (or planning for doing so in the appropriate season), or making a place of honor in your home for the Blessed Mother.

• RECIPE •

Salmon a la Dill

My friend Dorothy Radlicz shares her salmon recipe. Please don't shy away from serving fish to your kids. It is very healthy for them, and you might even be surprised by their response.

Dorothy loves to cook nutritious meals. She says, "I am first generation 100% Swiss, and good food cooked from scratch was my upbringing and how our boys, Andrew (24) and Christopher (23), were brought up. My husband is first generation 100% Polish, so he appreciated good food, having grown up with a mom who like my mom was a great cook."

Dorothy took the whole family cooking experience further: "Believing our boys should be able to cook good, wholesome food in their adult lives caused me to alternate cooking dinner with each of them during the summers. My mom also used to cook with them and make special items for the holidays during their younger years. We also sent them to the Culinary Institute of America (CIA) in Hyde Park, New York, for a few classes."

Ingredients

- Fresh salmon fillet (3–4 lbs.)
- ½ cup sour cream
- ¼ cup plain yogurt
- ¼ cup mayonnaise
- 2 tbsp. Dijon or stone-ground mustard
- 1 tsp. dried dill
- 1 cup fresh cucumber, very thinly sliced
- 1 tbsp. lemon juice, freshly squeezed
- salt and paprika

Directions

Place sliced fresh cucumber in a bowl and sprinkle with salt. Let sit for thirty minutes. This will cause the cucumber to drain some of its juice. Discard juice. Sprinkle the top side of the fresh salmon fillet with lemon juice, then evenly spread on mustard and sprinkle with dill. Grill or bake salmon fillet (at about 425°F) until cooked through (or to your preference). Cooking time depends on the thickness of your salmon. A one-inch-thick piece will grill in about 8 to 10 minutes and will bake in 15 to 30 minutes. Salmon is done when it is easily flaked with a fork. Remove cooked salmon and place on platter. Mix sour cream, yogurt, and mayonnaise together. Add cucumber. Spread cucumber mixture across top of salmon fillet. Sprinkle paprika on top of the cucumber mixture, down the center of salmon fillet.

You can serve this dish immediately or refrigerate it and serve it chilled. Everyone will love it! Enjoy!

FORTY-EIGHT
Learning About Our Duty to Be a Good Example from John A. Hardon, SJ

CONTEMPLATE

You are the salt of the earth; but if salt has lost its taste, how can its saltiness be restored? It is no longer good for anything, but is thrown out and trampled under foot. You are the light of the world. A city built on a hill cannot be hid. No one after lighting a lamp puts it under the bushel basket, but on the lampstand, and it gives light to all in the house. In the same way, let your light shine before others, so that they may see your good works and give glory to your Father in heaven.

—Matthew 5:13–16 (NRSV)

PREPARATIONS

Decide in advance if you'll enlist helpers to assist with making dinner and for help with setting the table. If time allows, read the Contemplate passage and think about it during the day. Also, read the Dinner Table Teaching in advance of your dinner time.

You might consider breaking this lesson up into two dinners, since it is a little longer than other teachings, but it can be done in one teaching.

OPENING PRAYER
(to be read out loud by parent or guardian or by all)

Dear Lord, Jesus, please visit our family, blessed with one another and with food to eat. Please take care of those who are lacking in food and do not have a family. *Grace Before Meals. Hail Mary.*

DINNER TABLE TEACHING
Read the Contemplate passage and this Dinner Table Teaching out loud to the family.

We have a duty always to give a good example to others. In the Gospel of Matthew, after Jesus teaches the disciples the Beatitudes, which are the eight conditions for happiness for this life and the next, St. Matthew then quotes three parables from Jesus. He uses the images of salt of the earth, light of the world, and light on a lampstand to drive home the lessons in the Beatitudes. Let's take them one at a time.

We are to be salt of the earth. This is true for every Christian but most especially those who are in a teaching authority, such as parents, teachers, and church leaders. John A. Hardon, SJ, Servant of God, is a former friend and spiritual director of mine, now deceased. (His cause for canonization has been opened.) Fr. Hardon said: "We must above all preserve ourselves as the salt which keeps far away the corruption of error and of moral evil; we much communicate to others the savor of the true spirit of Christ."[36]

We are the light of the world. Jesus Christ spoke of Himself as being the Light of the World. As Christians we share in this privilege and huge responsibility. Christ came to teach truth to the world. He calls baptized

Christians to proclaim his truth. Fr. Hardon taught: "We are to be communicators of the Truth, who is Christ, by everything we say and do, in fact by everything we are. People are to see, in us, Christ on earth today."[37]

We are the lampstand in the house. The "house" is our domestic church, our neighborhoods and communities, our Catholic Church, and even the whole world. We start first within our homes as Mother Teresa often taught: "Love begins at home." Jesus asks us to be sure that we don't hide our light. Additionally, he instructs us: "Let your light shine before others, so that they may see your good works and give glory to your Father in heaven" (Matt. 15:16 NRSV). After our duties to family, friends, and neighbors, Fr. Hardon reminds us of our duty to be a good example to society, too: "God made us members of a society, and we therefore have duties toward others in society. We need them, and they need us. And on no level is this need greater than to witness to the Christ in whom we believe and whose disciples we claim to be."[38]

You might let your "salt" become stale by getting a bit lazy. Or you may fail to let your light shine because of various strains and pressures of life. Or you might hide your light, feeling your gifts are not significant. But Jesus calls us to set a good example and bring others to Him through our lives of love. Fr. Hardon says, "People are to see, in us, Christ on earth today."[39]

REFLECTION QUESTIONS
Ask the children to share their thoughts.

What does Jesus want you to do with your gifts?

How can you be a light to others? List three ways.

Do you ever hide your light "under a bushel"? If so, why? And what can you do to let your light shine?

Why is prayer important in this regard?

CLOSING PRAYER

(to pray together out loud)

Grace After Meals. Jesus, help me to use my gifts for Your glory. *Our Father.*

Look over the optional activities below and discuss with the family to see if you can carry them out during the upcoming week.

WEEKDAY PRAYER

Each day of the upcoming week at the dinner table, pray this simple prayer.

Dear Lord, Jesus, open my heart to Your love. Grant me all of the graces I need to set a good example always. Amen.

THEME EXTENSION

This activity is for anyone in the family, or it can be carried out together.

Get out a pen and paper and list the gifts you believe God gave you. What are you good at doing? Are you using your gifts? What can you do to give glory to God and help others? I recommend that you do this activity together as a family so that individual gifts can be reinforced by other family members.

EXTRA CREDIT!

This activity is for the entire family.

Sometime this week, take a few moments to try to become more aware of the gifts that God has given to you. Discuss with the family at the dinner table this week a way in which you can use the gifts within your family to help teach someone about Jesus. Take it a step further, if possible, and discuss what you can do for someone in your neighborhood or community.

FORTY-NINE
The Gifts of the Holy Spirit

CONTEMPLATE

The seven gifts of the Holy Spirit are wisdom, understanding, counsel, fortitude, knowledge, piety, and fear of the Lord. They belong in their fullness to Christ, Son of David. They complete and perfect the virtues of those who receive them. They make the faithful docile in readily obeying divine inspirations.

—CCC 1831

PREPARATION

Decide in advance if you'll enlist helpers to assist with making dinner and for help with setting the table. If time allows, read the Contemplate passage and think about it during the day. Also, read the Dinner Table Teaching in advance of your dinner time.

OPENING PRAYER
(to be read out loud by parent or guardian or by all)

Dear Lord, Jesus, please visit our family, blessed with one another and with food to eat. Please take care of those who are lacking in food and do not have a family. *Grace Before Meals. Hail Mary.*

DINNER TABLE TEACHING

Read the Contemplate passage and this Dinner
Table Teaching out loud to the family.

The seven gifts described in Isaiah 11:2–3 are imparted by the Holy Spirit and are higher than the theological or cardinal virtues because they bring divine assistance as opposed to acting within the limits of human ability. The gifts of the Holy Spirit are wisdom, understanding, counsel, fortitude, knowledge, piety, and fear of the Lord. Let's take them one at a time.

1. **Wisdom** is considered the highest gift. It helps us to keep God central in our lives and to see the importance of others. It helps us to see things from God's perspective. It inspires contemplative reflection.

2. **Understanding** is the ability to comprehend God's message. Understanding goes farther than faith because it gives insight into belief.

3. **Counsel** enables us to judge promptly and rightly the best way to follow God's plans when we are faced with choices.

4. **Fortitude** is firmness of spirit—the courage to do what is right. This gives us steadiness of will in doing good despite any opposition and obstacles.

5. **Knowledge** lets us explore and ponder God's revelation and recognize that there are mysteries of faith far beyond us. It perfects the virtue of faith and helps us discern between impulses of temptation and inspirations of grace.

6. **Piety** helps us pray to God with devotion. It perfects the virtue of justice, infusing us with a loving and affectionate obedience to God the Father.

7. **Fear of the Lord** instills in us a profound respect for the glory and power of the all-present God, whose friendship we never want to lose. When we pray an Act of Contrition sincerely, we express a fear of the Lord.

REFLECTION QUESTIONS

Ask the children to share their thoughts.

Who imparts the seven gifts of the Holy Spirit to you?

List three reasons why the gifts are important.

Should you pray to the Holy Spirit for the gifts?

Name one way that a gift of the Holy Spirit can work in your heart.

CLOSING PRAYER

(to pray together out loud)

Grace After Meals. Holy Spirit, please enlighten us and grant us Your gifts. *Our Father.*

———

Look over the optional activities below and discuss with the family to see if you can carry them out during the upcoming week.

WEEKDAY PRAYER

Each day of the upcoming week at the dinner table, pray this simple prayer.

Dear Lord, Jesus, open my heart to Your love. Holy Spirit, help me to become more aware of Your gifts. Amen.

Also, pray this prayer:

Fr. Hardon's Prayer to the Holy Spirit for an Increase in the Gifts

O Lord Jesus Christ, who before ascending into heaven, you promised to send the Holy Spirit to finish your work in the souls of your apostles and disciples, deign to grant the same Holy Spirit to me that He may perfect in my soul the work of your grace and love. Grant me the spirit of wisdom that I may despise the perishable things of this world and aspire only after those which are eternal, the spirit of understanding to enlighten my mind with the light of your divine truth, the spirit of counsel that I may ever choose the surest way of pleasing God and gaining heaven, the spirit of fortitude that I may bear my cross with you and overcome with courage all the obstacles that oppose my salvation, the spirit of knowledge that I may know God and myself and grow perfect in the science of the saints, the spirit of piety that I may find the service of God sweet and amiable, the spirit of fear that I may be filled with a loving reverence toward God and dread in any way to displease Him. Mark me, dear Lord, with the sign of your true disciples and animate me in all things with your spirit. Amen.[40]

THEME EXTENSION

This activity is for anyone in the family, or it can be carried out together.

Take the time to pray to the Holy Spirit, asking for His help.

EXTRA CREDIT!

This activity is for anyone in the family.

Sometime this week, take a few moments to help organize some of your family recipes and put them in a recipe box or notebook.

FIFTY
The Cardinal Virtues

CONTEMPLATE

Four virtues play a pivotal role and accordingly are called "cardinal"; all the others are grouped around them. They are: prudence, justice, fortitude, and temperance. "If anyone loves righteousness, [Wisdom's] labors are virtues; for she teaches temperance and prudence, justice, and courage." These virtues are praised under other names in many passages of Scripture.

—CCC 1805

PREPARATIONS

Decide in advance if you'll enlist helpers to assist with making dinner and for help with setting the table. If time allows, read the Contemplate passage and think about it during the day. Also, read the Dinner Table Teaching in advance of your dinner time.

OPENING PRAYER
(to be read out loud by parent or guardian or by all)

Dear Lord, Jesus, please visit our family, blessed with one another and with food to eat. Please take care of those who are lacking in food and do not have a family. *Grace Before Meals. Hail Mary.*

DINNER TABLE TEACHING

Read the Contemplate passage and this Dinner
Table Teaching out loud to the family.

There are four cardinal virtues. Let's take them one at a time, as the *Catechism* explains them.

"Prudence is the virtue that disposes practical reason to discern our true good in every circumstance and to choose the right means of achieving it; 'the prudent man looks where he is going'" (CCC 1806).

"Justice is the moral virtue that consists in the constant and firm will to give their due to God and neighbor. Justice toward God is called the 'virtue of religion.' Justice toward men disposes one to respect the rights of each and to establish in human relationships the harmony that promotes equity with regard to persons and to the common good" (CCC 1807).

"Fortitude is the moral virtue that ensures firmness in difficulties and constancy in the pursuit of the good. It strengthens the resolve to resist temptations and to overcome obstacles in the moral life. The virtue of fortitude enables one to conquer fear, even fear of death, and to face trials and persecutions. It disposes one even to renounce and sacrifice his life in defense of a just cause" (CCC 1808).

"Temperance is the moral virtue that moderates the attraction of pleasures and provides balance in the use of created goods. It ensures the will's mastery over instincts and keeps desires within the limits of what is honorable. The temperate person directs the sensitive appetites toward what is good and maintains a healthy discretion: 'Do not follow your inclination and strength, walking according to the desires of your heart'" (CCC 1809).

REFLECTION QUESTIONS

Ask the children to share their thoughts.

List two ways that you use the virtue of prudence in daily life.

How can you use the virtue of justice in your family?

How does fortitude help you?

Why should a faithful Catholic strive to use the virtue of temperance?

CLOSING PRAYER

(to pray together out loud)

Grace After Meals. All of the angels and saints, please pray for us. *Our Father.*

Look over the optional activities below and discuss with the family to see if you can carry them out during the upcoming week.

WEEKDAY PRAYER

Each day of the upcoming week at the dinner table, pray this simple prayer.

Dear Lord, Jesus, open my heart to Your love. Help me to put the virtues into practice each day. Amen.

THEME EXTENSION

This activity is for anyone in the family.

Reflect on becoming more attentive about practicing the virtues in your daily life. As a difficulty or challenge emerges, pause to pray and strive to put a virtue into practice.

EXTRA CREDIT!

This activity is for anyone in the family.

Sometime this week, take a few moments to unplug from technology and spend some extra time with family members. You can even set a timer if needed.

FIFTY-ONE
The Theological Virtues

CONTEMPLATE

The theological virtues are the foundation of Christian moral activity; they animate it and give it its special character. They inform and give life to all the moral virtues. They are infused by God into the souls of the faithful to make them capable of acting as his children and of meriting eternal life. They are the pledge of the presence and action of the Holy Spirit in the faculties of the human being. There are three theological virtues: faith, hope, and charity.

—CCC 1813

PREPARATIONS

Decide in advance if you'll enlist helpers to assist with making dinner and for help with setting the table. If time allows, read the Contemplate passage and think about it during the day. Also, read the Dinner Table Teaching in advance of your dinner time.

OPENING PRAYER
(to be read out loud by parent or guardian or by all)

Dear Lord, Jesus, please visit our family, blessed with one another and with food to eat. Please take care of those who are lacking in food and do not have a family. *Grace Before Meals. Hail Mary.*

DINNER TABLE TEACHING

Read the Contemplate passage and this Dinner
Table Teaching out loud to the family.

A virtue, first of all, is a habitual and firm disposition to do good. All human virtues are rooted in the theological virtues, which relate to God. The three theological virtues are faith, hope, and charity. We receive these powerful virtues as gifts from God when we are baptized, and they give life and meaning to our moral acts. The Holy Spirit works through these virtues. As St. Gregory of Nyssa says, "The goal of a virtuous life is to become like God."[41]

The *Catechism* teaches, "**Faith** is the theological virtue by which we believe in God and believe all that he has said and revealed to us, and that Holy Church proposes for our belief, because he is truth itself. By faith 'man freely commits his entire self to God'" (CCC 1814).

"**Hope** is the theological virtue by which we desire the kingdom of heaven and eternal life as our happiness, placing our trust in Christ's promises and relying not on our own strength, but on the help of the grace of the Holy Spirit" (CCC 1817).

"**Charity** is the theological virtue by which we love God above all things for his own sake, and our neighbor as ourselves for the love of God" (CCC 1822).

As mentioned above, we receive the theological virtues at Baptism, but we must exercise them throughout our lives by using them. We also can pray for them to increase. It's important to understand that the theological virtues are gifts from God, while cardinal virtues are virtues we acquire by human effort.

REFLECTION QUESTIONS

Ask the children to share their thoughts.

When do you receive the theological virtues?

What are the three theological virtues?

What do these virtues help us to do?

Can you list some ways that you can grow in virtue?

CLOSING PRAYER

(to pray together out loud)

Grace After Meals. All of the angels and saints, please pray for us. *Our Father.*

———

Look over the optional activities below and discuss with the family to see if you can carry them out during the upcoming week.

WEEKDAY PRAYER

Each day of the upcoming week at the dinner table, pray this simple prayer.

Dear Lord, Jesus, open my heart to Your love. Help me to become a more virtuous person. Amen.

THEME EXTENSION

This activity is for anyone in the family.

Each time you feel temped to take the easy way out of something (a chore or responsibility), pause and pray, and then try even harder to accomplish your goal.

EXTRA CREDIT!

This activity is for anyone in the family.

Sometime this week, take a few moments to examine your conscience and your life. Think about whether you are practicing the virtues in your life, or if you are letting them go stagnant and unused.

FIFTY-TWO
Learning About Redemptive Suffering from St. John Paul II and the Saints

CONTEMPLATE

Therefore, uniting myself with all of you who are suffering in your homes, in the hospitals, the clinics, the dispensaries, the sanatoria—wherever you may be—I beg you to make use of the cross that has become part of each one of you for salvation. I pray for you to have light and spiritual strength in your suffering, that you may not lose courage but may discover for yourselves the meaning of suffering and may be able to relieve others by prayer and sacrifice.

—St. John Paul II[42]

PREPARATIONS

Decide in advance if you'll enlist helpers to assist with making dinner and for help with setting the table. If time allows, read the Contemplate passage and think about it during the day. Also, read the Dinner Table Teaching in advance of your dinner time.

OPENING PRAYER
(to be read out loud by parent or guardian or by all)

Dear Lord, Jesus, please visit our family, blessed with one another and with food to eat. Please take care of those who are lacking in food and do not have a family. *Grace Before Meals. Hail Mary.*

DINNER TABLE TEACHING
Read the Contemplate passage and this Dinner Table Teaching out loud to the family.

Catholics and Christians have a different way of looking at suffering than the rest of the world. The saints have often revealed the mysterious beauty and graces interwoven in suffering. The Church teaches that there is much value in our suffering if we lovingly unite it with and offer it to Jesus. Ponder St. John Paul II's words above on the mystery of redemptive suffering. In the apostolic letter *Salvifici Doloris,* he says, "In suffering there is concealed a particular power that draws a person interiorly close to Christ, a special grace."[43]

Many times we may think we are smarter than God—that we know exactly what we need. St. Paul said, "A thorn was given me in the flesh, a messenger of Satan to torment me, to keep me from being too elated. Three times I appealed to the Lord about this, that it would leave me, but he said to me, 'My grace is sufficient for you, for power is made perfect in weakness'" (2 Cor. 12:7–9 NRSV). Recognizing the great lesson in weakness and the power in God's divine mercy, St. Paul continued, "Therefore I am content with weaknesses, insults, hardships, persecutions, and calamities for the sake of Christ; for whenever I am weak, then I am strong" (2 Cor. 12:10 NRSV).

Knowing of a deep personal suffering that I was enduring, Mother Teresa once wrote in a personal letter to me: "Jesus shares His love with you and shares His suffering and pain. He is a God of love and does not want His children to suffer, but when you accept your pain, suffering, death, and resurrection your pain becomes redemptive for yourself and for others. . . . Be assured of my prayers. Christ calls us to be one with Him in love through unconditional surrender to His plan for us. Let us allow Jesus to use us without consulting us by taking what He gives and giving what He takes."

All throughout our Christian lives we have many opportunities to offer up our inconveniences, challenges, and sufferings, asking Jesus to redeem them and bring good out of them for our own souls and for those in our midst, especially for those who have harmed us or are opposing us. Redemptive suffering can work miracles in human hearts!

REFLECTION QUESTIONS
Ask the children to share their thoughts.

What can be good about suffering?

What do you think Jesus meant when He instructed, "If any want to become my followers, let them deny themselves and take up their cross and follow me" (Mk. 8:34 NRSV)?

How can praying help us when we are suffering illness or pain?

CLOSING PRAYER
(to pray together out loud)

Grace After Meals. St. John Paul II, St. Teresa of Calcutta, and all the saints, please pray for us. *Our Father.*

———

Look over the optional activities below and discuss with the family to see if you can carry them out during the upcoming week.

WEEKDAY PRAYER

Each day of the upcoming week at the dinner table, pray this simple prayer.

Dear Lord, Jesus, open my heart to Your love. Help me to offer my heart more fully to You when I am suffering in some way. Amen.

You may also add the following prayer:

Fatima Prayer

(The Blessed Mother taught this prayer to the three child visionaries to pray when offering up penances, sufferings, and sacrifices.)

Oh my Jesus, I offer this for love of Thee, for the conversion of sinners, and in reparation for the sins committed against the Immaculate Heart of Mary.

THEME EXTENSION

This activity is for anyone in the family.

Pray the Fatima Prayer of reparation for the conversion of sinners (above) any time you'd like to offer something up to Jesus.

EXTRA CREDIT!

This activity is for anyone in the family.

Sometime this week, take a few moments to reflect upon St. Thérèse of Lisieux's words:

I understood that to become a saint one had to suffer much, seek out always the most perfect thing to do, and forget self. I understood, too, that there are many degrees of perfection and each soul was free to respond to the advances of the Our Lord, to do little or much for Him, in a word, to choose among the sacrifices He was asking. Then, as in the days of my childhood, I cried out: "My God, *I choose all!*" I do not want to be a *saint by halves.* I'm not afraid to suffer for You. I fear only one thing: to keep my own will; so take it, for I choose all that You will![44]

• RECIPE •

Apple Cinnamon Baked French Toast

My friend Barb Scholten shares this fun and delicious recipe for apple cinnamon baked French toast. It is similar to another recipe in this book for overnight Christmas pecan-blueberry French toast. But this recipe contains fresh apples and cinnamon.

Barb and her family first enjoyed a dish like this when staying at a bed and breakfast. She now loves to make it herself. Barb's family really enjoys having friends over for Sunday brunch after Mass along with family. "This is our go-to recipe," she says, "as it is made the night before, and we can set the oven to bake it while we are at church! The house smells lovely when we arrive, and brunch is ready to put on the table." Add a fruit bowl, and precooked bacon or sausage. "We just start the coffee and tea, and relax and enjoy each other!"

Ingredients
- 6–8 apples
- 1 loaf French bread (Barb uses whole grain)
- 8 large eggs
- 3½ cups milk
- ¾ cup sugar (divided)
- 1 tbsp. vanilla
- 3 tsp. cinnamon
- ½–1 tsp. nutmeg (depending on your preference)
- 1 tbsp. butter

Directions

Cut bread into one-inch slices. Grease or spray a 9 x 13–inch glass pan. Place bread in dish, with the pieces tightly fitting together.

In a large bowl, beat eggs, ½ cup sugar, milk, and vanilla with a whisk for about 30 seconds. Pour *half* of the egg mixture over the bread slices.

Core and slice apples fairly thin. (Barb uses organic, so she does not peel the apples, but you may choose to peel them.) Place sliced apples on top of the bread, overlapping apple slices in rows, so it looks very nice and orderly. Then pour the rest of the egg mixture over the apple slices.

Mix the remaining ¼ cup of sugar with cinnamon and nutmeg, and sprinkle it evenly over apples. Dot with the 1 tbsp. butter, cut into small pieces. Cover and refrigerate overnight.

Next day: Preheat oven to 350°F. *Uncover* dish and bake 1 hour. It will rise and brown nicely. (Note: you may cook it at 325°F for 1½ hours if necessary.)

Remove from oven; let it rest for 10 minutes. Cut into squares and serve with pure maple syrup. Enjoy!

FIFTY-THREE
(EXTRA CREDIT!)
Angels

CONTEMPLATE

He will command his angels concerning you to guard you in all
your ways. On their hands they will bear you up, so that you will
not dash your foot against a stone.

—Psalm 91:11–13 (NRSV)

PREPARATIONS

*Decide in advance if you'll enlist helpers to assist with making dinner and
for help with setting the table. If time allows, read the Contemplate passage and
think about it during the day. Also, read the Dinner Table Teaching in advance
of your dinner time.*

OPENING PRAYER
(to be read out loud by parent or guardian or by all)

Dear Lord, Jesus, please visit our family, blessed with one another and
with food to eat. Please take care of those who are lacking in food and do
not have a family. *Grace Before Meals. Hail Mary.*

DINNER TABLE TEACHING

Read the Contemplate passage and this Dinner
Table Teaching out loud to the family.

God created the angels to assist and protect humankind. They have been given the special mission of delivering God's messages to human beings. Angels are messengers, adorers of God, guardians of God, ambassadors of God, guides, and mediators. Even as the angels adore God in heaven, they pray and help us spiritually on our heavenward journey.

"Are not all angels spirits in the divine service, sent to serve for the sake of those who are to inherit salvation?" (Heb. 1:14 NRSV). Angels are pure, invisible spirits, and we find them mentioned in both the Old and New Testaments—from the beginning to the very end of the Bible. Yet we may overlook the world of angels because they are invisible! We should get to know the angels, who were created by God before the physical universe and humankind.

St. John Paul II presented a series of talks on angels, collected as the "Catechesis on the Holy Angels."[45] He points out that the reality of angels was denied in Christ's time by the Sadducees and has been denied in every age since then. Yet many saints have taught about the angels, and some, including St. Padre Pio and St. Catherine Labouré, have had the privilege of seeing their guardian angels.

There is a guardian angel to help each person get to heaven. St. Thomas Aquinas believed they do this by enlightening our minds with holy ideas. Theologian and Servant of God John Hardon, SJ, explains it this way: "These pure Spirits most nearly resemble God and yet are not dissimilar to man, having intelligence and will like us. They are God's intermediaries between the God they see and mankind whom they are entrusted to lead to the same Beatific Vision."[46]

REFLECTION QUESTIONS
Ask the children to share their thoughts.

Why did God make the angels?

How can the angels help you?

Can you talk to your guardian angel?

Extra credit (since the answer cannot be found in the teaching above): What is the name of the angel who visited the Blessed Virgin Mary to tell her God's plan for her?

CLOSING PRAYER
(to pray together out loud)

Grace After Meals. All of the angels and saints, please pray for us. *Our Father.*

———◆———

Look over the optional activities below and discuss with the family to see if you can carry them out during the upcoming week.

WEEKDAY PRAYER
*Each day of the upcoming week at the dinner
table, pray this simple prayer.*

Dear Lord, Jesus, open my heart to Your love. Show me ways to come closer to You. Remind me of the guardian angel in my life. Amen.

Also, pray this prayer:

Angel of God,
my guardian dear,

To whom God's love
commits me here,
Ever this day,
be at my side,
To light and guard,
Rule and guide.
Amen.

THEME EXTENSION
This activity is for anyone in the family, or it can be carried out together.

Try to learn more about the holy angels. Do a little research and see if you can find some things that St. Padre Pio, St. Francis de Sales, St. Ambrose, and St. John Paul II have said about the angels.

On September 29 the Church observes a special feast day for the archangels Michael, Raphael, and Gabriel. On October 2 we observe a special feast day for the holy guardian angels. Try to celebrate these special feast days of the angels by saying prayers to the angels and perhaps enjoying a special dessert together.

EXTRA CREDIT!
This activity is for the entire family.

Sometime this week, take a few moments to get in touch with a relative and arrange for a time in the near future to gather for a meal.

ACKNOWLEDGMENTS

I am deeply grateful to my parents, Eugene Joseph and Alexandra Mary Cooper, for bringing me into the world and raising me in a large Catholic family. To my brothers and sisters—Alice Jean, Gene, Gary, Barbara, Tim, Michael, and David—thank you for being a part of my life.

My heartfelt gratitude goes to my husband, Dave, and my beloved children—Justin, Chaldea, Jessica, Joseph, and Mary-Catherine—for their continued love and support, and to my grandson, Shepherd. I love you all dearly!

I am extremely thankful for my readership, viewership, and listenership and to all those I meet in my travels. I pray for you every day. Thank you for being part of my fascinating journey through life! I pray that God will continue to bless you in great abundance. Please pray for me, too.

Finally, I owe special thanks to Paraclete Press—to Robert Edmonson, Phil Fox Rose, and all of the wonderful team.

ABOUT THE AUTHOR

In addition to her passion for cooking and gathering the family together around the dinner table as a Catholic wife, mother of five children, and grandmother, Donna-Marie Cooper O'Boyle is an award-winning and best-selling author and journalist, TV host, speaker, and retreat leader. She is the EWTN television host of *Everyday Blessings for Catholic Moms* and *Catholic Mom's Cafe*, which she created to teach, encourage, and inspire Catholic mothers. She loves children and has been a catechist for almost thirty years and an extraordinary Eucharistic minister to the sick and to her parish. Donna-Marie was noted as one of the Top Ten Most Fascinating Catholics in 2009 by *Faith & Family Live*. She enjoyed a decade-long friendship with Mother Teresa of Calcutta and became a Lay Missionary of Charity. For many years her spiritual director was Servant of God John A. Hardon, SJ, who also served as one of Mother Teresa's spiritual directors.

Donna-Marie was invited by the Holy See in 2008 to participate in an international congress for women at the Vatican to mark the twentieth anniversary of the apostolic letter *Mulieris Dignitatem* (On the Dignity and Vocation of Women). She received apostolic blessings from St. John Paul II and Pope Benedict XVI on her books and work and a special blessing from St. John Paul II for her work with St. Teresa of Calcutta, or Mother Teresa. Donna-Marie has received awards for her work including a Catholic Press Award for her book *Catholic Mom's Cafe*, First Place Award from Connecticut Press Club for her book *Mother Teresa and Me*, and First Place Award from The National Federation of Press Women for *Mother Teresa and Me*, and the Media Award from the American Cancer Society for a volunteer column she wrote for the newspaper.

Donna-Marie is the author of over twenty books on faith and family, including *Rooted in Love: Our Calling as Catholic Women*, *The Miraculous Medal: Stories, Prayers, and Devotions*, *Mother Teresa and Me: Ten Years of Friendship*, *The Domestic Church: Room By Room*, *My Confirmation Book*, *Catholic Mom's Cafe: 5-Minute Retreats for Every Day of the Year*, *Angels for Kids*, and her memoir *The Kiss of Jesus: How Mother Teresa and the Saints Helped Me to Discover the Beauty of the Cross*.

Donna-Marie has been featured by Zenit news and *Rome Reports* and is a frequent guest on EWTN television: *Bookmark*, *Sunday Night Prime*, *Women of Grace*, *Faith & Culture*, and *Vatican Insider*, as well as a frequent guest on national radio. Donna-Marie lives with her family in beautiful rural Connecticut, admiring God's creation. Learn more about Donna-Marie's books and ministry at her website: www.DonnaCooperOBoyle.com.

NOTES

1 St. Teresa of Calcutta, Mother Teresa of Calcutta Center, accessed May 2, 2016, www.motherteresa.org/05_prayers/prayer-fam.html#2.

2 Benedict XVI, *Porta Fidei: An Apostolic Letter Issued "Motu Proprio," for the Indiction of the Year of Faith* (St. Peter's: 2011).

3 Vatican Council II, *Lumen Gentium: The Dogmatic Constitution on the Church, Promulgated by Pope Paul VI* (November 21, 1964), 11.

4 Ibid.

5 St. Teresa of Calcutta, quoted in Malcolm Muggeridge, *Something Beautiful for God: Mother Teresa of Calcutta* (London: Collins, 1971), 112.

6 Paul VI, *Solemni hac Liturgia (Credo of the People of God): An Apostolic Letter Issued "Motu Proprio"* (St. Peter's: 1968), 30.

7 Jill Haak Adels, *The Wisdom of the Saints: An Anthology* (New York: Oxford University Press, 1987), 130.

8 Donna-Marie Cooper O'Boyle, *The Miraculous Medal: Stories, Prayers, and Devotions* (Cincinnati, OH: Servant Books, 2013), 26.

9 St. Josemaría Escrivá, *Christ Is Passing By* (Chicago: Scepter Press, 1974), 56.

10 St. Teresa of Ávila, *The Life of Teresa of Jesus*, trans. E. Allison Peers (New York: Image, 1991), 35.

11 St. Maria Faustina Kowalska, *Diary: Divine Mercy in My Soul* (Stockbridge, MA: Marian Press, 1987), 180.

12 Ibid., 47.

13 Ibid.

14 Ibid., 1158.

15 John Paul II, "Mary Was United to Jesus on the Cross," *L'Osservatore Romano* (Weekly Edition in English, November 1, 1995), 11.

16 John Paul II, "Mary's Place Is Highest After Christ," *L'Osservatore Romano* (Weekly Edition in English, January 10, 1996), 11.

17 John Paul II, *Gift and Mystery: On the Fiftieth Anniversary of My Priestly Ordination* (New York: Doubleday, 1996).

18 St. Gregory of Nyssa, *Homilies on the Beatitudes*, Homily 1, 82.23.

19 U.S. Catholic Bishops, *Sharing Catholic Social Teaching: Challenges and Direction: Reflections of the U.S. Catholic Bishops* (Washington, DC: United States Catholic Conference, 1998), introduction.

20   "Teresa Avila Quotes," The Order of Carmelites, accessed May 2, 2016, http://ocarm.org/en/content/ocarm/teresa-avila-quotes.

21   Ibid.

22   Vatican Council II, *Sacrosanctum Concilium: The Constitution on the Sacred Liturgy, Promulgated by Pope Paul VI* (December 4, 1963), 47.

23   Vatican Council II, *Lumen Gentium: The Dogmatic Constitution on the Church, Promulgated by Pope Paul VI* (November 21, 1964), 11.

24   In this and the subsequent chapters, the form of the Ten Commandments is the "Traditional Catechetical Formula" from "The Ten Commandments," *Catechism of the Catholic Church*, Part 3, Section 2.

25   Congregation for the Doctrine of the Faith, *Donum Vitae: Instruction on Respect for Human Life* (February 22, 1987), introduction, 5.

26   St. Teresa of Calcutta speaking at National Prayer Breakfast (Washington, DC, February 5, 1994), accessed May 2, 2016, www.catholicnewsagency.com/resources/abortion/catholic-teaching/blessed-mother-teresa-on-abortion.

27   "Pope Benedict XVI's Prayer for the Unborn," EWTN, accessed May 2, 2016, www.ewtn.com/Devotionals/prayers/b16_unborn.htm.

28   Pope Francis, "Homily at Canonization Mass of Four Saints" (St. Peter's: October 18, 2015).

29   "Thérèse: Life Story: Her Parents," Society of the Little Flower, accessed May 3, 2016, www.littleflower.org/therese/life-story/her-parents.

30   Ibid.

31   St. Teresa of Ávila, *Life of Prayer*, ch. 3.

32   St. Augustine of Hippo, *Confessions*, bk. 1, ch. 1

33   Vatican Council II, *Dei Verbum: De Divina Revelatione: The Dogmatic Constitution on Divine Revelation of Vatican Council, Promulgated by Pope Paul VI* (November 18, 1965), 11.

34   John Paul II, *Gift and Mystery: On the Fiftieth Anniversary of My Priestly Ordination* (New York: Doubleday, 1996).

35   Ibid.

36   John A. Hardon, SJ, "The Spiritual Teaching of Christ: Maxims of the Spiritual Life Based on the Parables of Christ," Father John A. Hardon, S.J., Archives (Inter Mirifica, 2004), accessed May 3, 2016, www.therealpresence.org/archives/Sacred_Scripture/Sacred_Scripture_002.htm, 9.

37   Ibid.

38   Ibid.

39   Ibid.

40   John A. Hardon, SJ, "The Work of the Holy Spirit in the Church and in the World: Prayer," Father John A. Hardon, S.J. Archives, (Inter Mirifica, 1998), accessed May 3, 2016, www.therealpresence.org/archives/Holy_Spirit/Holy_Spirit_001.htm.

41   St. Gregory of Nyssa, *Homilies on the Beatitudes*, Homily 1, 82.23.

42   John A. Hardon, SJ, "Martyrdom & Suffering: Redemptive Suffering—John Paul II and the Meaning of Suffering," Father John A. Hardon, SJ, Archives, (Inter Mirifica, 1998), accessed May 3, 2016, http://www.therealpresence.org/archives/Martyrs/Martyrs_006.htm.

43   John Paul II, *Salvifici Doloris, An Apostolic Letter on the Christian Meaning of Human Suffering* (St. Peter's: 1984), 26.

44   St. Thérèse of Lisieux, *The Story of a Soul*, 27.

45   John Paul II, "Catechesis on the Holy Angels by Pope John Paul II, Given at 6 General Audiences from 9 July to 20 August 1986," EWTN Libraries, accessed May 12, 2016, www.ewtn.com/library/PAPALDOC/JP2ANGEL.HTM.

46   John A. Hardon, SJ, "Angelology—Angels in Heaven, on Earth and in Hell," Father John A. Hardon, S.J., Archives (Inter Mirifica, 1998), accessed May 12, 2016, http://www.therealpresence.org/archives/Angelology/Angelology_007.htm.

ABOUT PARACLETE PRESS

WHO WE ARE

Paraclete Press is a publisher of books, recordings, and DVDs on Christian spirituality. Our publishing represents a full expression of Christian belief and practice—from Catholic to Evangelical, from Protestant to Orthodox.

We are the publishing arm of the Community of Jesus, an ecumenical monastic community in the Benedictine tradition. As such, we are uniquely positioned in the marketplace without connection to a large corporation and with informal relationships to many branches and denominations of faith.

WHAT WE ARE DOING

PARACLETE PRESS BOOKS | Paraclete publishes books that show the richness and depth of what it means to be Christian. Although Benedictine spirituality is at the heart of who we are and all that we do, we publish books that reflect the Christian experience across many cultures, time periods, and houses of worship. We publish books that nourish the vibrant life of the church and its people.

We have several different series, including the best-selling Paraclete Essentials and Paraclete Giants series of classic texts in contemporary English; Voices from the Monastery—men and women monastics writing about living a spiritual life today; our award-winning Paraclete Poetry series as well as the Mount Tabor Books on the arts; best-selling gift books for children on the occasions of baptism and first communion; and the Active Prayer Series that brings creativity and liveliness to any life of prayer.

MOUNT TABOR BOOKS | Paraclete's newest series, Mount Tabor Books, focuses on the arts and literature as well as liturgical worship and spirituality, and was created in conjunction with the Mount Tabor Ecumenical Centre for Art and Spirituality in Barga, Italy.

PARACLETE RECORDINGS | From Gregorian chant to contemporary American choral works, our recordings celebrate the best of sacred choral music composed through the centuries that create a space for heaven and earth to intersect. Paraclete Recordings is the record label representing the internationally acclaimed choir Gloriæ Dei Cantores, praised for their "rapt and fathomless spiritual intensity" by *American Record Guide*; the Gloriæ Dei Cantores Schola, specializing in the study and performance of Gregorian chant; and the other instrumental artists of the Gloriæ Dei Artes Foundation.

Paraclete Press is also privileged to be the exclusive North American distributor of the recordings of the Monastic Choir of St. Peter's Abbey in Solesmes, France, long considered to be a leading authority on Gregorian chant.

PARACLETE VIDEO | Our DVDs offer spiritual help, healing, and biblical guidance for a broad range of life issues including grief and loss, marriage, forgiveness, facing death, bullying, addictions, Alzheimer's, and spiritual formation.

Learn more about us at our website:
www.paracletepress.com or phone us
toll-free at 1.800.451.5006

SCAN
TO
READ
MORE

OTHER BEST-SELLING TITLES
by Donna-Marie Cooper O'Boyle

Angels for Kids
ISBN 978-1-61261-408-3
$14.99 Paperback
The invisible world of angels is so often overlooked, though it has been present since before the dawn of Creation, offering attentive service and protection to humankind. Based on Catholic teaching, *Angels for Kids* offers proof of the true existence of angels while dispelling prevalent contemporary myths.

My Confirmation Book
ISBN 978-1-61261-357-4
$16.99 Hardcover
Part keepsake, part teaching book, this small volume is filled with inspiration, encouragement, and reflections to ponder for fourth-graders and up. Through simple text, it explains the privileges and responsibilities imparted through the sacrament of Confirmation.

Available from most booksellers or through Paraclete Press:
www.paracletepress.com | 1-800-451-5006
Try your local bookstore first.